Birds of Trinidad and Tobago

Birds of Trinidad and Tobago
Second Edition

Text by Richard ffrench
Photographs by Roger Neckles

MACMILLAN
CARIBBEAN

Macmillan Education
Between Towns Road, Oxford OX4 3PP
A division of Macmillan Publishers Limited
Companies and representatives throughout the world

www.macmillan-caribbean.com

ISBN 978-0-333-99584-6

First published 1986

Second edition 2004

Typeset by CjB Editorial Plus
Illustrated by Tessa Eccles
Cover design by Gary Fielder, AC Design
Cover photographs by Roger Neckles

Printed and bound in Malaysia

2016 2015 2014 2013 2012
12 11 10 9 8

Contents

Map of Tobago

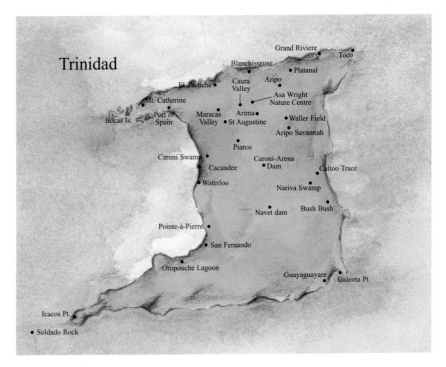

Map of Trinidad

Preface

This book treats 106 species of birds, mostly the more common ones, from Trinidad and Tobago; about 40 of these are also found in the eastern Caribbean. There is a brief introduction which covers the basic facts about local birds: the numbers of families and species that may be found in Trinidad and Tobago; their relationships to birds of the mainland and other islands; migration; habitats; ecology. The parts of a bird are described and habits, such as flocking, feeding, roosting, nesting, display, rivalry, parasitism and predation are discussed. Information is given about how to watch birds, the equipment needed, photography and conservation. Advice on where to go in Trinidad and Tobago to see birds is included (with maps). Finally, a short bibliography is given at the end of the Introduction.

The text divides the birds into eight groups according to their habitats: gardens and parks; open country and scrubland; cultivated land with large trees; the forest; swamps, marshes and reservoirs; the coast; the air (comprising those species most commonly seen soaring or feeding in the sky); the night (including those birds normally active only at night).

Each species is treated similarly. Both the English and the scientific names are given, and some local names are included. The length and a simple field description are given for each bird. Where appropriate, details of voice, habitat and range, and migratory habits are noted. Details of diet, habits, roosting and/or nesting are also given, along with any unusual aspects of behaviour.

Each species is illustrated by a colour photograph, taken on location in Trinidad or Tobago. Where male and female of a species differ in appearance, the sex of the bird in the photograph is given in the caption.

Introduction

Among the islands of the West Indies, Trinidad and Tobago provide a fascinating opportunity for anyone interested in natural history, particularly birds. Trinidad's position – a mere 10 miles distant from the South American mainland – means that its flora and fauna are essentially continental in nature. The great variety of species that is typical of the South American region is also present in Trinidad and, to a lesser degree, in Tobago.

In addition, the position of the islands, at the southern end of the Antillean island chain, means that many northern migratory birds stay or pass through on their way to wintering grounds in the south. Furthermore, several southern species migrate north from Argentina to Venezuela or the Guianas during the austral winter, and some of these regularly visit Trinidad and Tobago.

Although both islands are small, they contain a wide variety of habitats, including tropical rain forest, swamp forest, semi-deciduous forest, mangrove swamp, freshwater marshland, coastal fringes and savannah, as well as cultivated lands. Some of these habitats are not very extensive, but each is large enough to support a distinct population of birds.

As a result of these factors, the number of bird families and species which are found on the two islands is quite large in relation to their size. Over 425 species from 65 families have been recorded in Trinidad, while over 230 species are known in Tobago. Over 250 species breed in Trinidad, and about 100 in Tobago. Altogether, more than 450 species are listed for both islands, some 25 of which are known only on Tobago.

A somewhat larger number of species is recorded for the rest of the West Indies – including the Bahamas. Many of the Antillean islands have comparatively few species but, because of their small size, their isolation and their restricted habitat, these tend to include a high proportion of endemic species. By contrast, Trinidad has only one endemic species, and Tobago has none. But recent DNA studies of several forest species have indicated the possibility of some degree of endemism on both islands.

As mentioned earlier, migrants form a significant proportion of the birds of Trinidad and Tobago. The great majority – about 100 species – come from their breeding grounds in the north. Most arrive between August and October, some passing through after a brief or perhaps extended rest, the others staying during the northern winter months. In about April they return north, many species travelling further to the west on the return journey. A few of these northern visitors, especially some waterbirds, may remain on Trinidad or Tobago during the mid-year period; probably most are immature birds, not yet ready to breed.

Fewer species – about 40 in all – visit from the south, but some of these breed in nearby Venezuela, so their migration to our islands is just a temporary dispersal of population. These southern visitors may arrive as early as January and most of them have left by September.

Ecology

It is important for the student of birds to recognise the relationship between the habitat of a species and its life history. Clearly, a bird will live in a place in which it can find the food that suits it, and it

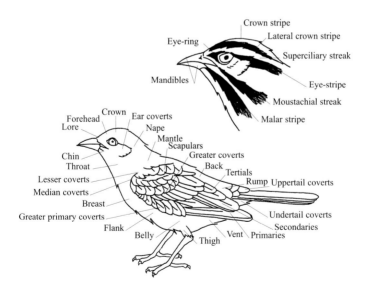

will nest where suitable material and a site can be found. Thus, in the study of birds one needs to learn more than the mere details of plumage and voice; attention should also be paid to the precise details of where the bird feeds and what it feeds on.

With knowledge of these details, one can eventually build up a thorough understanding of a bird's environment and needs. This can even help in identification, since a particular species is highly unlikely to be found in an unsuitable habitat. A positive identification may be made by realising that only one of the species fitting a description is likely to be found in that habitat.

Describing birds

It is helpful to know the correct terms which are used to describe the parts of a bird (see page 2).

In this book, the average length of an adult (from beak to tail) is given in both centimetres and inches. Where appropriate, the wingspan (from wing tip to wing tip) of a flying bird is included.

The habits of birds

The habits of birds are particularly interesting and can usually be observed quite easily. A few of the most noticeable habits are described below.

- **Flocking.** Some species like to congregate in flocks when feeding, flying or roosting. These flocks may be very large, as in the case of roosting grackles, or quite small, as in a family party of anis. Flocking can be an advantage to a species as a defence against an enemy or as a means of communicating information about food. However, flocking is by no means universal; some birds never form a group larger than an individual family.

- **Diet.** Understanding a bird's diet involves the knowledge of how it obtains its food, which can be a fascinating area of study in itself. For example, an insect-eater may catch flying insects in mid-air, pick them up from the ground, find them inside tree-holes or under bark, search for them on the undersides of leaves, or dig down into soil or mud to extract them. As a group, birds feed on flesh, fish, molluscs, worms, reptiles, invertebrates, eggs, fruit, leaves, seeds and nectar – and on each other. However, individual species are often very specific in their diet, so a captive bird which is given unsuitable food may die without touching it.

- **Sleep.** Little is known about the sleeping habits of birds; they seem to just disappear when darkness approaches. Many people mistakenly assume that at night birds return to their nests; this is generally only the case for an incubating or brooding parent during the nesting period (the Bananaquit being a notable exception). It is likely that many species find shelter amidst vegetation or in a tree-hole, and sleep there. Some prefer to roost collectively, and the study of such communal roosting, as in Scarlet Ibis, Cattle Egrets and frigatebirds, can be very interesting.

- **Breeding and display.** Breeding behaviour in birds can be quite complex and each species tends to conform to a particular pattern. There are many different ways in which birds select their partners, establish a breeding territory, choose a nest-site and build a nest, lay and incubate the eggs, and feed and care for the young. Nests themselves vary immensely in form, even within Trinidad and Tobago. These include not only the well-known cup-shaped type, but also, among others, spheres with side entrances, bags, tubes, mounds and hammocks; some birds build no nest at all, or merely construct a 'token' nest at the site where they lay their eggs. The nest-sites and materials used are also extremely varied. Some young are precocial, that is, they are capable of leaving the nest and feeding themselves within a few hours of hatching. Others remain in the nest, helpless and entirely dependent on parental attention during the fledging period which may last from nine days (in small finches) to more than three months (in the Oilbird).

One of the most interesting facets of breeding behaviour concerns the manifestations of rivalry and advertisement, usually called display. The male attracts the attention of his mate, or stimulates her towards sexual activity, by displaying particularly colourful parts of his plumage or other physical attributes. Occasionally, the female may join him in a mutual display; she rarely initiates the behaviour. The song of a male bird is a type of display, and is often associated with display movements. Forms of display vary almost as much as plumage, and are sometimes so specific that they can become an aid to identification of the bird. Certain displays are aimed more at impressing or intimidating rival males. Some male birds, such as manakins and hermit hummingbirds, congregate to display together.

These displays are known as leks. Several examples of this behaviour occur in Trinidad and Tobago, and some have formed the subjects of very interesting studies.

- **Feathers.** The delicate balance and precision needed for efficient aerial manoeuvre require that a bird maintains its feathers in the best possible condition; therefore, birds continually preen themselves, not only for hygiene, but also to ensure the correct positioning of feathers, particularly the flight feathers. They use their oil glands to help preserve waterproofing. In addition to normal wear, the feathers may also suffer damage, so all feathers are regularly shed and renewed by the process of moulting, which, in the case of most local birds, occurs once a year. Since moulting birds are sometimes handicapped by the absence of one or more flight feathers, it is not surprising to find that the moult period usually occurs *after* a breeding season which is a time in which parent birds are required to be especially active to feed and care for their young. Birds may be more than usually quiet and subdued during their moulting period, so are less likely to be seen then.

- **Inter-specific relations.** Inter-specific relations among birds also form a subject of interest. Certain species feed on others, and these predatory birds, such as hawks, falcons and owls, include some of the most spectacular and attractive birds in the country. Perhaps we are less inclined, emotionally, to appreciate the way in which certain species steal the eggs or nestlings of other birds, but it is of course all part of Nature's infinitely varied design. A most intriguing form of predation is shown in the parasitic behaviour of some birds, e.g. frigatebirds, which literally steal food from the mouths of others, or appropriate their nests (before they have completed their breeding cycle), or even, as in the case of the cowbirds and some cuckoos, deposit eggs in other birds' nests, for the hosts to incubate and nurture.

Watching birds

It may be useful to lay down certain principles for the aspiring bird-watcher – often nowadays called a birder – to follow in order to make the best use of the available opportunities. Obviously it helps if you know the best way to approach birds; you also need to know where to go from there.

A birdwatcher must try to be inconspicuous, to avoid alarming birds he or she is watching. Therefore, he or she must wear suitable clothing, keep as quiet as possible and move as little as possible. Many birds soon become familiar with a stationary object, so losing the inhibitions that normally cause them to fly away. When walking in the forest or in thick cover, it is especially important to be silent because forest birds are very aware of sound, which is their own principal means of communication.

In the tropics, it is particularly important to look for birds either in the first half of the morning or during the last two hours of daylight. Many birds, especially those in open areas, tend to stay under cover, where it is cooler, during the hot, middle hours of the day. Probably the best time for birdwatching is between 6 a.m. and 9 a.m.

Although it is not essential to use binoculars or a telescope for birdwatching, these aids will improve your view and enable you to see and recognise much that would otherwise escape your notice. There are many types of binoculars, and a wide price range reflecting the varied quality. Beginners should avoid binoculars that are too heavy, since one needs to cultivate rapid coordination of eye and hand for the best results. The most convenient size is 8 × 30, but 7 × 35 or 8 × 40 will also do. Those with magnification of 10 × are often difficult to keep steady. A telescope is best used with a tripod over a fixed field of view, such as mudflats, marshes or the sea. But remember that, in the tropics, heat haze often obscures low level viewing.

Just as important a piece of equipment is the notebook. There is no substitute for making your own notes, if you want to remember details accurately. It also ensures that you record what you actually *see* and/or *hear* – if you make it a rule to make your own notes *before* checking a guidebook for help in identification. Notes should be as full as is convenient, and, ideally, they should include details of plumage, size, call-notes, behaviour, habitat, location, time and conditions when sighted. If you cannot include all of the above, a few notes are better than none. Here it is useful to share your birdwatching experiences with a companion, since this tends to lessen the chances of errors in observation. This is particularly important where rare birds are concerned. In Trinidad and Tobago it is possible to communicate with other birders via the Southeastern Caribbean Bird Alert, which can be reached on the internet (www.wow.net/ttfnc). Information on birding activities and how to report rarities can be done through this organisation, which is linked with the Trinidad and Tobago Field Naturalists' Club, founded in 1891, which arranges excursions and publishes its own newsletters and journals.

A word of warning about bird photography. Although photographs of birds can be useful and decorative, they can also be extremely difficult to obtain. It has been said that you can't be a good birdwatcher and a bird photographer at the same time, as the two activities tend to exclude each other. Certainly photographers should be careful not to put their own interest in getting a good bird picture before the safety and welfare of their subject. This is especially important with nesting birds, which are liable to desert their nests if disturbed.

Where to watch birds in Trinidad and Tobago

There are many good locations for birdwatching in our islands (see maps, page vi). To see swamp and marsh birds in Trinidad you should go to Caroni Swamp (access is possible by boat from the northeastern corner of the swamp, adjoining the highway) or to nearby marshes at Cacandee or the rice fields east of the highway. Nariva Swamp is also a good place to see marsh birds, but is less accessible. The edges may be approached at Caltoo Trace, the boat trail leading west to Bush-Bush, and further south at Kernahan Trace. Oropouche Lagoon is particularly rewarding in the wet season; access can be gained from the Pluck–La Fortune road.

Trinidad's Northern Range has many access points, too numerous to mention here, along the roads and trails that go up the various valleys. Outstanding areas are the Arima Valley, including the Asa Wright Nature Centre, Las Lapas Trace and the Maracas and Caura Valleys which have trails leading to El Tucuche. The Aripo and Cumaca roads lead to interesting locations on the slopes of Mount Aripo and in the Platanal. Different birds may be found in the northwest, at Mount Catherine, or on the Bocas Islands. Forest birds of a different kind may also be found in the low lying areas of Arena, Guayaguayare and the oil fields in the south and southwest.

Reservoirs and mudflats are always good places to see waterbirds. If you are fortunate enough to be able to visit any of the major dams, e.g. Navet or Caroni-Arena, or the Pointe-à-Pierre reservoirs, you stand a good chance of seeing some interesting birds. For mudflats, probably the best places to visit are the coast at

Waterloo on the west coast, also the Caroni rice fields, where in season large numbers of migrant shorebirds and others congregate.

Certain species thrive well in suburban habitats; you should go to Pointe-à-Pierre, St Augustine or the cities of Port of Spain or San Fernando to see these. But birds need vegetation, of course, so they will be found in such places as parks or golf courses. The Queen's Park Savannah and Botanic Gardens in Port of Spain provide the right habitat for a number of species.

Savannah birds are best found on large areas of open ground, such as Waller Field, Aripo Savannah and Piarco, but in the dry season you will not see many because most will have moved to nearby marshland. Many savannah birds seem to associate to some extent with cattle, so cattle ranches often contain some interesting bird life.

To see seabirds off the coast of Trinidad you will need to visit the Gulf of Paria (especially at Waterloo), Toco, Nariva river mouth or Galeota Point. However, the seabird enthusiast must visit Tobago, which is the home of many more species that nest at several locations. These locations include St Giles Islands and Little Tobago, both of which are bird sanctuaries with restricted access. Seabirds may also be found close to shore at Store Bay, Buccoo, and Plymouth on the west coast, and at Scarborough and Smith's Island on the east.

Other good birdwatching areas in Tobago include the Hillsborough Dam district, Grafton Estate, the Roxborough–Bloody Bay road (especially at Gilpin Trace) and Charlotteville. Swamp and marshland in Tobago are limited, but some species can be found at Bon Accord, and especially at Buccoo marshes, which can be reached from Buccoo village via some pasture land.

The above is by no means a complete list of the best sites for birdwatching, but it does provide some suggestions for the beginner. You will soon establish your own favourite spots.

Some useful references

A Guide to the Birds of Trinidad and Tobago, 2nd edn. (1991). Richard ffrench. Cornell University Press, New York.

Birds of the West Indies (1998). Herbert Raffaele *et al.* Helm, London.

A Guide to the Birds of Venezuela, 2nd edn. (2003). Steve L. Hilty. Princeton University Press, New Jersey.

The North American Bird Guide. David Sibley (2000) Chanticleer Press, Inc., New York.

Nature Trails of Trinidad. Richard ffrench and Peter Bacon (revised V. Quesnel) (1992). S. M. Publications, Port of Spain.

Living World. The Journal of the Trinidad and Tobago Field Naturalists' Club. Published approx. every two years.

1 Gardens and Parks

◆ Blue-gray Tanager   *Thraupis episcopus*

Length: 17 cm (7 inches)   **Family:** Tanagers

One of the most well-known and popular birds in the country, this species, known locally as 'Blue Jean', is found chiefly in cultivated areas and suburban districts, as well as in light woodland and forest edges. Blue-gray Tanagers are often seen around houses and gardens, flying about in noisy and restless groups. Generally bluish grey in colour, the upperparts are brighter blue and there is a vivid violet-blue patch on each wing covert. The Tobagan birds are darker and more brilliantly coloured than their Trinidadian counterparts. The call-notes are a series of squeaky, high-pitched sounds without a regular pattern.

Blue-gray Tanager

The Blue-gray Tanager feeds on fruits of many kinds, including tomatoes and other commercially grown vegetables; it also takes insects, either from the air or from amidst foliage, and readily comes to feeding tables for fruit or bread. Breeding is mainly between March and July, and nests are usually high up in trees. The eggs are incubated for 14 days; the fledging period is 17 days.

◆ Palm Tanager　　　　　*Thraupis palmarum*

Length: 17 cm (7 inches)　　　　　　**Family:** Tanagers

This species is so closely related to the Blue-gray Tanager that some people think that they may in fact be the same species with two colour morphs. Some individuals show distinctly bluish upperparts and are possibly hybrids with the Blue-gray Tanager. Like the Blue-gray, the Palm Tanager inhabits cultivated areas and suburban districts; but, true to its name, it seems to favour palms and generally feeds at a higher level above ground. Known locally as 'Palmiste', it is common on Trinidad and has recently colonised Tobago, where it is becoming steadily more common. Generally dull olive-green, it has yellowish wing coverts and dark primaries, so in flight it appears to have a pale wing bar. The song is almost indistinguishable from that of the Blue-gray.

Palm Tanager

It feeds on fruit, nectar and insects by foraging among palms and other trees which have small berries, often hanging upside down from large palm leaves. It also frequents feeding tables in gardens. Nests are built in palms or under the eaves of houses, even on the beams of verandah roofs. This is a restless bird, which is full of 'nervous energy'.

◆ White-lined Tanager *Tachyphonus rufus*

Length: 18 cm (7 $\frac{1}{2}$ inches)   **Family:** Tanagers

Sometimes called the 'Parson', this attractive and lively bird is common on both islands in suburban districts and at the edge of forests. Superficially resembling a cowbird, the male is glossy black all over, except for the underwing coverts and a small patch on the upper coverts which are white (visible only when the bird is flying). In addition the bill is sharper and more pointed than the cowbird's, and the lower mandible is whitish at the base. The female is entirely rufous brown. As the pair frequently associate together they may easily be identified. The song is a musical repeated phrase.

This species feeds largely on fruit and nectar, but insects are also eaten; it is often attracted to overripe fruit on bird tables. The nest is a large cup of leaves, usually situated in thick vegetation, some-times in a garden shrub. The eggs are whitish and beautifully marked with dark brown.

◆ Bananaquit *Coereba flaveola*

Length: 10 cm (4 inches)   **Family:** Bananaquits

Known locally as 'Sucrier' or 'Sugarbird', this species must be one of the most abundant to be found on both islands; indeed it is probably the most widespread and common species throughout the majority of the islands of the West Indies. It lives in almost every type of habitat: high mountains, rain forests, suburban and cultivated areas; even along the edges of mangrove swamps and sea coasts. Its extreme abundance is partly due to its frequent breeding. It is a tiny bird, which is variable in plumage. On our islands the adult is black above with white superciliary streaks and wing patches; the rump and most of the underparts are bright yellow. The short, black bill is slightly decurved. The song is a squeaky chatter.

Feeding principally on nectar, this bird may be readily attracted

White-lined Tanager ♂

Bananaquit

by sugar, syrup or overripe bananas, and as a result may become exceedingly tame, for example in many hotel dining rooms. It builds a conspicuous nest: a sphere made of grass and leaves with a side entrance protected above by a 'porch'. Apart from the usual nest, which is constructed for breeding, Bananaquits also build 'sleeping' nests which are more roughly made. These nests are placed in a variety of sites, ranging from the lower tree branches to artificial situations such as mailboxes. The adult birds often seem to be compulsive nest builders, even starting to build a new nest quite close to the previous one.

◆ Tropical Mockingbird — *Mimus gilvus*

Length: 25 cm (10 inches)   **Family:** Mockingbirds

A comparatively recent (early twentieth century) arrival to Trinidad, this species is now widespread in suburban areas on both islands. It seems to be spreading into open countryside and even into clearings on the edge of forests. It is less common in mountainous regions but is frequently found amidst the deciduous light forest of offshore islands. Unmistakable in appearance, it is grey above with

Tropical Mockingbird

dark eye-streaks, white superciliary streaks and whitish underparts; most conspicuous is the long, white-tipped tail. It is an indefatigable and attractive singer, especially in the early morning when it is one of the first birds to sing. In Tobago the Tropical Mockingbird is known as 'Day Clean'.

An extremely aggressive species, it will not tolerate other birds of any species on its territory, and will chase and fight intruders until victorious. In gardens, owls, hawks, snakes, large lizards, mongooses, and even domestic animals may be attacked. The nest is a large, untidy cup of sticks, often placed in a low tree or bush. The three blue eggs are spotted with brown.

◆ Great Kiskadee   *Pitangus sulphuratus*

Length: 22 cm (9 inches)   **Family:** Tyrant Flycatchers

This is probably the best-known bird in Trinidad, but it is not normally found in Tobago. It is widespread in suburban gardens and open country with scattered trees, and may also be seen in

Great Kiskadee

Barred Antshrike ♂

Copper-rumped Hummingbird

mangrove swamps or on the edge of forests. The upperparts are dark brown, as are the wings which are edged with rufous. The head is black (apart from a concealed yellow crest that is raised only in moments of excitement) with a broad white streak around it. The underparts are mostly bright yellow, and the bill is heavy and strong. Though very similar to the Boat-billed Flycatcher (*Megarhynchus pitangua*) in appearance, Kiskadees may always be distinguished by their well-known cry, *Kis-ka-dee*.

This bird feeds on almost anything, but especially large insects and berries and it readily comes for scraps. The nest is a large untidy ball of grass with a side entrance, and is usually situated conspicuously in a tree or wedged against a telephone pole. The adults resolutely defend the area against all enemies.

◆ Barred Antshrike   *Thamnophilus doliatus*

Length: 15 cm (6 inches)   **Family:** Antbirds

This engaging, dumpy little bird is often seen in suburban gardens and light woodland on both islands, where its trusting nature frequently brings it into contact with humans. It is less commonly found at forest edges or at higher altitudes up to 600 metres (2000 feet). In most antbirds the sexes differ from each other in appearance, the males being predominantly black and the females brown. In this species the male is barred black and white all over; it has a noticeable crest and a short tail. The female is largely chestnut brown and is also crested. Many antbirds keep in contact with each other by calling frequently. In this species the call is a chuckling series, *ka-ka-ka*, etc., accelerating towards the end; while calling, the bird wags its tail rapidly in time with the notes.

This antbird tends to skulk in low bushes, and its flight is short and rather weak. It feeds on small insects and is rarely seen high in trees. The nest is a flimsy hammock, suspended below a fork in a small plant, where both sexes incubate the eggs in turn and care for the young. Two spotted eggs are laid.

◆ Copper-rumped Hummingbird   *Amazilia tobaci*

Length: 10 cm (4 inches)   **Family:** Hummingbirds

Of all the 17 members of this family that are known in our islands, this is the most commonly seen on both islands. It is found in a variety of habitats, from gardens and open country to cultivated lands and the edge of forests, even up to 600 metres (2000 feet). The sexes are similar in appearance: mainly brilliant iridescent green above and below, with coppery bronze on the lower back and tiny white tufts at the thighs; the bill is of medium length and straight. Apart from a twittering call and a single *tsip*, given while feeding, this species has a recognisable song, a series of three or four high pitched notes, e.g. *tee-tee-tyu*.

Being very aggressive in defence of its territory, this humming-bird will attack any other bird, especially early in the year during its breeding season. Its nest is a small cup of plant-down which is usually placed on a small branch, but sometimes it is attached to wires or to another unlikely object. Incubation and fledging last for five weeks or more.

◆ Black-throated Mango *Anthracothorax nigricollis*

Length: 11 cm (4½ inches)   **Family:** Hummingbirds

Black-throated
Mango ♂

This bird is wide ranging on both islands. It can be seen in gardens, in open country with scattered trees and at the edges of forest, from sea-level to mountain ridges. It seems to be largely absent from September to December, possibly because some birds migrate to the continent. One of the larger hummers, this species is bronze-green above with a purple tail. Males are black below with iridescent blue bordering the throat; females are white below with a prominent black stripe from chin to abdomen. The fairly long bill is slightly decurved.

It feeds on small insects, which are often caught in flight, and on the nectar of a wide variety of plants. The nest is a cup built of plant-down and decorated with lichen, which probably helps to camouflage the nest, which is usually placed in an open position on a thin branch quite high in a tree. Males display by spreading their colourful tails wide as they perch, so that the light shines through the feathers.

◆ Smooth-billed Ani

Length: 30 cm (12 inches)

Crotophaga ani

Family: Cuckoos

Smooth-billed Ani

Known locally as 'Merle Corbeau' or even as 'Old Witch', this bird inhabits open country, gardens, parks and urban areas in both islands. Black all over, it is distinguished by its strange, parrot-shaped beak, its short, rounded wings and its long tail, which it raises to balance itself on landing. Its commonest call is a whining, two-tone *oo-leek*.

Anis, like other cuckoos, live mostly on grasshoppers and other insects. They are not parasitic in their nesting behaviour, but they are highly gregarious, feeding and living together in flocks of about 12 birds; they even nest in one large communal nest, where the females in the group may deposit up to 30 chalky white eggs. Several birds may incubate together, and the young are fed and guarded by all the adults in the group, as well as by the subadult birds from previous broods. A larger species, the Greater Ani, *Crotophaga major*, inhabits mainly marshes or swamps.

◆ Eared Dove   *Zenaida auriculata*

Length: 22 cm (9 inches)   **Family:** Pigeons and Doves

This species is fairly common in the more open areas, especially on Tobago, but on Trinidad it is more confined to savannahs and

Eared Dove

marshes. It is probably a partial migrant, for numbers seem to increase during the wet season, when it may be seen in small flocks. It is a medium-sized pigeon, generally greyish brown with conspicuous black spots on the wing coverts; it also has black markings on the sides of the head, with an iridescent violet patch beside its ears. Although the sexes are roughly similar, the female is duller on the whole. Its call is a typical pigeon's cooing.

Like many of this family, this dove feeds on the ground mainly on seeds; it has learned also to take bread from bird tables and has become quite tame in parts of Tobago. It breeds in most months of the year, constructing a small nest of twigs which is placed usually quite low in a tree, often a mangrove at a swamp edge. The two white eggs are incubated by both parents, and the time for incubation and fledging together is little more than three weeks.

◆ Carib Grackle — *Quiscalus lugubris*

Length: 26 cm (10 $\frac{1}{2}$ inches)   **Family:** Orioles and Blackbirds

Generally known as 'Blackbird' or sometimes 'Boat-tail', this species is smaller than similar members of the family that are found in North America or the Greater Antilles. The male is a glossy purplish black with a long, keel-shaped tail; his bill is quite long and

Carib Grackle

decurved, and his eyes are white. The female is similar but smaller and with a more regular tail. Immatures are brownish black with brown eyes. The call-notes are remarkable, being a series of harsh clucks and squeaks, often ending with a ringing bell-like note. Although the species is known throughout the Lesser Antilles, its dialect from Grenada and Barbados northwards can readily be distinguished from that of our islands.

Common in urban and suburban areas, the grackle sometimes feeds on grain and other seeds on open savannahs and rice fields; it also takes many harmful insects. It readily comes to feeding tables for scraps. A highly gregarious species, it nests in small groups and roosts in massive numbers, notably among the Caroni mangroves.

◆ Yellow Oriole   *Icterus nigrogularis*

Length: 20 cm (8 inches)   **Family:** Orioles and Blackbirds

By far the most common of the three oriole species that occur on Trinidad, this species, sometimes known as the Small Cornbird, is widespread in suburban areas, in open woodland and along the edges of mangrove swamps. Generally bright yellow with black lores, tail and throat, the adult sometimes has a golden head (thus its other name, Golden Oriole). The wings are black with white edges. Immature birds are dull yellow and lack most of the black features. The call varies from a harsh repeated *cack*, uttered mostly in alarm, to a beautiful, fluting song of several musical notes, often heard early in the morning.

It feeds largely on insects and other invertebrates, taken from among foliage, but also eats berries, small fruits, and nectar from a variety of flowering shrubs and trees. The nest is a pendulous tube of grass or palm fibres, about 45 cm (18 inches) long with the entrance hole near the top. It is slung from a branch of medium height. Sometimes the Piratic Flycatcher (*Legatus leucophaius*) forces the orioles to abandon their nest, but they usually just build another close by.

◆ House Wren   *Troglodytes aedon*

Length: 13 cm (5 inches)   **Family:** Wrens

One of the most familiar little birds in our islands, this wren is often known as 'House Bird' since it is frequently found around houses, moving like a mouse surreptitiously about the roof, walls, windows

Yellow Oriole

House Wren

and drains in search of the small insects and spiders which form its principal diet. It is generally brown, slightly paler on the under-parts and has a short tail, sometimes cocked up. Like many wrens, it compensates for its cryptic appearance by singing quite loudly a lengthy, trilling phrase, which it sometimes repeats many times at short intervals. It is also known to forage for food in churches, prompting the nickname 'God-bird', as its song competes for attention with the priest!

Since it builds its nest in tree-holes and other cavities, this wren is often found nesting around houses and outbuildings at any time of year. The nest is a comparatively large, rather untidy cup of sticks lined with various soft materials (even discarded snake skins), where it lays up to six eggs. Incubation and fledging together last for about a month. As the nests are fairly conspicuous, it is not surprising that this wren is often parasitised by the Shiny Cowbird (see page 33).

2 Open Country and Scrubland

♦ **Fork-tailed Flycatcher**   *Tyrannus savana*

Length: 40 cm (16 inches)   **Family:** Tyrant Flycatchers

Most commonly found on savannahs and in open country, this species, locally called 'Scissors-tail', does occasionally visit the foothills of the Northern Range, as well as cultivated lands on ridges in Tobago. Two distinct populations are known on our islands: the common one migrates from Argentina and Chile, wintering in northern South America between May and October; the

Fork-tailed
Flycatcher

less common race, distinguished by its paler back, is seen between November and February. Neither has yet been found to breed locally. With grey upperparts, a black head and white underparts, this spectacular flycatcher is best distinguished by its extremely long outer tail feathers (28 cm or 11 inches in the male; 18 cm or 7 inches in the female). However, many birds moult these feathers between June and September, so are then seen without them; new ones gradually appear before the birds return south.

These flycatchers mainly feed in open country, perching on trees, bushes and fences, from which they fly out to seize their prey in flight. This is a very gregarious bird, especially at the roost (which is often in mangroves). The birds fly to the roost in vast, loose flocks from the surrounding district during the last hour of daylight. In this flight the birds spread out and travel at about 30 metres (100 feet) above the ground.

◆ Tropical Kingbird *Tyrannus melancholicus*

Length: 21 cm (8 ½ inches) **Family:** Tyrant Flycatchers

Frequently mistaken for a Kiskadee, this species lives on both islands in open country. It is often seen perching on the tops of bare trees and electrical or telephone wires. On Tobago it has a close relative, the Gray Kingbird (*Tyrannus dominicensis*) which rarely visits Trinidad. The Tropical Kingbird is duller in plumage than a Kiskadee, having a grey head with a dark eye-streak, grey to brown upperparts, and a pale throat and breast; the rest of the underparts are paler yellow than a Kiskadee's. The call is a high-pitched twittering, nothing like the Kiskadee's boisterous shout!

It feeds like a typical flycatcher, swooping out suddenly from its high perch to seize an insect in flight, and then returning to the original perch. Fearless in defence of its nest – an open cup of sticks placed usually high in a tree – the Kingbird attacks any other birds, including vultures and large hawks, that invade its territory. It is usually seen in pairs or alone.

◆ Southern Lapwing *Vanellus chilensis*

Length: 32 cm (13 inches) **Family:** Plovers

Although rare before 1970, this species has been steadily extending its range and its population. It has spread throughout both islands to areas of rough, muddy pastures with cattle, and is particularly

Tropical Kingbird

Southern Lapwing

common in Waller Field. Known throughout South America, it is common on the llanos, and seems now to be moving gradually into Central America. The Lapwing is a strikingly marked species with a crested head, black breast and black flight feathers with contrasting white coverts, making the bird spectacular in flight. Its call too is distinctive: a high-pitched series of raucous repeated notes, heard at night as well as by day. As it is one of the first species to react to danger, it acts as a sentinel for other species as well.

Breeding is now well established on both islands. The nest is merely a depression in the ground. As with all plovers, the young move away from the nest soon after hatching, their cryptic coloration making them hard to see on the ground. The food of this species comprises insects and other small arthropods.

Green-rumped Parrotlet

◆ Green-rumped Parrotlet　　*Forpus passerinus*

Length: 13 cm (5 inches)　　　　　　　　**Family:** Parrots

One of the smallest species in the parrot family, the 'Parakeet' or 'Lovebird' (as it is generally called) is now widespread in lowland areas of Trinidad, although it was not recorded before the twentieth century. It is less common in Tobago, where it may be an introduced species. A popular cage bird, this tiny parrot is bright green all over (with a brilliant blue wing patch in males) and has a pale pink bill. The call is a squeaky chatter and is usually heard in chorus.

This species is very gregarious and the birds are almost always seen in groups of 10 to 20. At night they congregate to roost in large numbers, and can often be seen preening each other's feathers as they settle for the night. The Parakeet flies with long undulating swoops, calling frequently in flight. It feeds on seeds and can cause damage to garden plants. It nests in a hole, exploiting not only natural cavities but also man-made structures, such as pipes and roof-eaves.

Ruddy Ground-Dove

◆ Ruddy Ground-Dove   *Columbina talpacoti*

Length: 17 cm (7 inches)   **Family:** Pigeons and Doves

In both islands, this must be one of the commonest and most successful species to inhabit open areas. It is found in suburban districts, waste land and, especially, in newly cleared forest land. The second largest of four ground-dove species, it is characterised by its short legs and generally reddish brown colouring. The male has a pale grey head and the female is a duller brown. In flight the black underwing coverts are noticeable. The call is a soft, rhythmical cooing, in which the first of two syllables is barely audible.

It feeds on seeds and is frequently seen walking on the ground in pairs. It breeds several times a year, building flimsy nests of grass or twigs that appear to be vulnerable to predation or natural disaster; these two competing factors presumably maintain a stable population. Rival males fight with their wings, and 'nervous' wing twitching is often seen in this species.

◆ Striped Cuckoo   *Tapera naevia*

Length: 25 cm (10 inches)   **Family:** Cuckoos

Striped Cuckoo

This bird, with the strange local name of 'Wife-sick', is known more for its prominent calls than for its appearance. It is usually found in low-lying open country with scattered trees and bushes, but is also sometimes found in clearings which border forest. Generally brown streaked with black above and paler below, it has a conspicuous white superciliary streak and a long tail. The usual call is a loud musical whistle of two or three notes, the second note pitched one semitone above the first; this call is repeated at intervals of several seconds and is made at night as well as by day. While calling, the bird raises its reddish brown crest.

This is the only one of the nine cuckoo species known to occur in Trinidad that is a brood parasite on other birds, like the well-known European species. Its eggs are always laid in the nests of one of the three spinetail species (see page 92), which are much smaller birds. Very little is known about how the cuckoo deposits its eggs in the spinetail's nest. Its food consists chiefly of insects and spiders.

◆ Ruby-topaz Hummingbird
Chrysolampis mosquitus

Length: 9 cm (3 $\frac{1}{2}$ inches)   **Family:** Hummingbirds

This species is common in open country and gardens on both islands, especially between January and July (many individuals

Ruby-topaz Hummingbird ♂

may migrate to the continent at other times). One of the most beautiful of our hummingbirds, the male is dark reddish brown with a green gloss; his crown and nape are brilliant iridescent red and his throat and breast are iridescent gold (these iridescent colours show only when the light catches them at the correct angle). Females and immatures are duller than adult males; they are brownish above and grey below with a short black stripe from chin to breast, and white tips on the outer tail. The bill is comparatively short and straight.

This hummingbird feeds on nectar taken from trees, such as samaan or fiddlewood, and from shrubs and small bushes in the garden such as *Russellia* or *Ixora*. The nest is a tiny cup of plant-down decorated with lichen, and is built usually in the fork of a small branch, which is often quite low in a tree or bush.

◆ Red-breasted Blackbird   *Sturnella militaris*

Length: 17 cm (7 inches)   **Family:** Orioles and Blackbirds

This is one of the most spectacular local birds. The male is sometimes known as the 'Soldier Bird' because of his brilliant scarlet throat and underparts. The rest of the male's plumage is blackish brown. The female's appearance is duller and paler with prominent

Red-breasted Blackbird ♂

buff streaks on the head, and a tinge of red about the breast. In Trinidad the species is only seen in savannahs and the drier marshlands; there are a few records from Tobago. The male's call is a short *chip*, followed by a long wheezing note, and is usually given during a display flight.

The Red-breasted Blackbird feeds largely on small invertebrates and seeds which are taken on the ground. The male often perches on a post or other prominent object. From here he flies up in a steep incline for about 8 metres (25 feet) in a display flight, returning with folded wings and showing off the brilliant scarlet plumage. The more cryptically coloured female builds her nest, a deep cup of grass, amidst long grass on the ground. However, although well hidden, it does not often escape the notice of the parasitic Shiny Cowbird.

◆ Shiny Cowbird   *Molothrus bonariensis*

Length: 18 cm (7 $\frac{1}{2}$ inches)   **Family:** Orioles and Blackbirds

Possibly a recent immigrant into the West Indies from South America, this species is a common resident of open country, including urban and suburban areas and farmland. The male is a brilliant bluish black, glossed with purple. Though resembling both the

Shiny Cowbird ♂

Grackle and the male White-lined Tanager, he can be distinguished by his brown eyes, shorter tail (often upturned), and shorter, dark, conical bill. The female is dull brown, and the immature is distinguished by a yellowish superciliary streak. The male's song is a beautiful series of loud, musical whistles, mixed with 'bubbling' notes.

The diet of the Shiny Cowbird is similar to that of the Grackle, with which it frequently associates at the roost. The local name, 'Lazy Bird', stems from its parasitic (and cuckoo-like) habit of laying eggs in other birds' nests. When hatched, the young cowbirds are fed and nurtured by their foster parents. Up to 20 species in Trinidad and Tobago are known to act as hosts to young cowbirds. The hosts' own young are usually unable to compete with the fast-growing cowbirds. Cowbird eggs are nearly spherical and they vary in size and colour. Several females may lay their eggs in the same nest.

◆ Blue-black Grassquit   *Volatinia jacarina*

Length: 10 cm (4 inches)   **Family:** Finches and Seedeaters

This species is abundant and well known on both islands. It has a variety of local names, including 'Ci-ci-zeb' and 'Johnny Jump-up'.

Blue-black Grassquit ♂

It inhabits savannahs and open areas, including the edges of mangroves, cane fields and suburban districts. It is almost always seen near the ground. The male's plumage is glossy black with a dark blue tinge and its beak is short and stubby. The female is dull brown and has pale brown underparts with blackish streaks. The call is a nasal wheeze, *jwee*.

A true grass bird, this species is usually seen feeding on grass seeds and, occasionally, insects. It feeds singly or in pairs, in rough ground. The nest is a small cup of grass which is placed low in a bush or in a clump of grass. The male performs an interesting display. He makes a short, upward jump from a perch (often a post or other vantage point) during which he spreads his wings and tail and utters the characteristic wheezing call. Then he lands back on the perch and repeats the performance every few seconds for quite some time.

◆ Northern Waterthrush   *Seiurus noveboracensis*

Length: 13 cm (5 inches)   **Family:** Wood Warblers

Twenty-four members of this family have been recorded on our islands, most of them only in very small numbers. Only three species are resident, but three others, including the Northern

Northern Waterthrush

Saffron Finch

Silver-beaked Tanager

Waterthrush, are common winter visitors from North America. This species is frequently found in light woodland near streams or rivers, mangroves or forest edge, between September and late April. Individuals are known to return to exactly the same places in subsequent 'winter' months. In appearance, it belies its name, hardly resembling a thrush except in its brown upperparts; its underparts are pale, heavily streaked with brown, and it has a conspicuous eyestripe. The call is a fairly loud, metallic single note, sounding like *tink*, and is often repeated.

Individuals feed alone, hunting for small invertebrates on the ground and amidst low vegetation. Frequently they toss aside leaves as they search for their prey. Mainly terrestrial, the bird walks busily about with a constant bobbing movement, somewhat resembling a sandpiper. One other thrush-like characteristic is its tendency to spend most of its time on the ground rather than in trees like most other members of its family.

◆ Saffron Finch   *Sicalis flaveola*

Length: 14 cm (5 $\frac{1}{2}$ inches)   **Family:** Finches and Seedeaters

This canary-like bird is common in parts of Trinidad. It is found on savannahs or semi-open country with large trees, especially on housing estates where close-cut lawns are abundant. The adult is bright yellow with an orange crown; it is more thick set and has a shorter, thicker beak than the otherwise similar Yellow Warbler. Immatures are generally grey, often with a pale yellow breast-band. The call is an incisive *chink*, and the song a musical phrase of several repeated notes.

The Saffron Finch feeds largely on grass seeds but also eats seeds of other plants. The nest is rarely built by the parents who prefer to use abandoned oriole nests, to the inside of which they add further material. However, occasionally the finches construct a cup nest in a tree-hollow or in one of a variety of artificial sites. Outside the breeding season (which is centred around August) many of these finches, especially the immatures, form loose flocks and feed in groups.

◆ Silver-beaked Tanager   *Ramphocelus carbo*

Length: 17 cm (7 inches)   **Family:** Tanagers

This species is common in Trinidad, but is not found in Tobago. It frequents light woodland and semi-open areas with bushy thickets.

It is also found on the edge of forests and in cultivated areas but rarely moves into the higher branches of trees. The male is outstandingly beautiful: a deep, velvety black, tinged with crimson especially around the head and breast. The bill is unusual, the upper mandible being black, while the lower one is bluish silver and much enlarged. The female is a duller reddish brown, and her bill is less enlarged. The call is a sharp metallic *chip*, and the song a rather squeaky musical phrase, repeated many times.

This tanager feeds mostly on fruit and nectar, especially from small shrubs and bromeliads close to the ground. Beetles, caterpillars and butterflies are also eaten. The bird nests during the first eight months of the year, building a deep cup of leaves which may be situated in a bush or amidst long grass. The eggs are bright blue with dark brown markings.

3 Cultivated Land with Large Trees

◆ **Rufous-browed Peppershrike**

Cyclarhis gujanensis

Length: 16 cm (6 ½ inches)

Family: Vireos

Far more commonly heard than seen, this species usually escapes our notice because it keeps to the thick foliage of trees and rarely moves close to the ground. The peppershrike flies rather weakly and only for short distances. It is common but is not found in Tobago. It usually inhabits light woodland and cultivated and suburban areas; less frequently, it is found in true forest or in mangroves. More robust than the other members of its family, it is green

Rufous-browed Peppershrike

above with a grey head and broad reddish superciliary streaks, and largely yellow underparts. The beak is powerful and hooked, so that it can tackle the hard outer casing of large beetles. The call is a very musical phrase of several notes in a set cadence, which is repeated every few seconds; although the tunes vary, the same one may be repeated unaltered as many as 200 times.

This species feeds on insects and spiders which it finds among thick foliage, mostly in the upper branches of trees. It breeds during the rainy season and the nest – which is rarely seen – is built high in a tree. The nest is a flimsy 'hammock', constructed of fine roots and moss, and slung in the fork of a branch.

◆ **Bare-eyed Thrush** *Turdus nudigenis*

Length: 24 cm (9 $\frac{1}{2}$ inches) **Family:** Thrushes

This well-known bird, also called the 'Gold-eye Thrush' or the 'Big-eye Grive', is widespread in both islands. It inhabits semi-open suburban areas with large trees, secondary forest and cultivated lands. It is less common at higher altitudes and not known at all in true rain forest. Mainly brown in colour, its lower underparts are pale grey, and its throat is streaked brown. Its most conspicuous feature is a large, bare, golden-yellow eye-ring, which gives it a strange staring appearance. Like many thrushes, it sings musically, but with less variety and power than most other Trinidadian thrushes. A common alarm note is a querulous, cat-like *keer-lee*.

This species feeds on a variety of soft fruits, insects and worms, mostly taken from the ground, and it readily comes for scraps. It nests during the early rainy season, building a substantial nest of mud and plant material, which is situated in the fork of a tree. Usually three eggs are laid; they are blue with dark brown spots.

◆ **Yellow-bellied Elaenia** *Elaenia flavogaster*

Length: 16 cm (6 $\frac{1}{2}$ inches) **Family:** Tyrant Flycatchers

This is one of the most common members of its family on both islands, but because of its nondescript appearance it frequently escapes notice. Sometimes known as 'Jay' or 'Cutterhead', it is found in light woodland, suburban gardens and on the edges of forest. The rather dull appearance of its greyish brown upper plumage is relieved by two white wing bars and pale greyish yellow underparts. Most prominent is its crest, which is almost always seen

Bare-eyed Thrush

Yellow-bellied Elaenia

raised. The Elaenia's call is a wheezing, drawn-out *zheer*. But at dawn it often sings a longer, rhythmical phrase persistently.

Elaenias feed on small insects, which may be caught in flight or hunted among foliage; they also take berries. The nest is usually built fairly high in a tree, and is a shallow cup of rootlets, decorated with lichen and often lined with feathers. Two spotted eggs are laid, and most of the parental duties are undertaken by the female parent.

◆ Cocoa Woodcreeper   *Xiphorhynchus susurrans*

Length: 23 cm (9 inches)   **Family:** Woodcreepers

Many people mistake these birds for woodpeckers, but in fact they can be distinguished by both their method of feeding and their morphology. This species is generally brown, streaked with buff above and below. The reddish tail is stiff and it acts as a prop when the bird climbs a tree (like a woodpecker). Its long, decurved bill is used as a probe and not to bore holes, and it never drums. The very penetrating call is a series of loud notes, *kew-kew-kew*, etc., which

Cocoa
Woodcreeper

tend to die away and to drop in pitch. Woodcreepers are found in forest and light woodland, including cultivated areas.

Feeding on invertebrates, woodcreepers not only probe tree bark and soft, rotten wood for their food, but also frequently follow army ants to feed on the insects and other creatures which are disturbed by the ants. They nest in tree-holes, normally using natural cavities or crevices; they do not bore nest-holes like woodpeckers.

◆ Golden-olive Woodpecker   *Piculus rubiginosus*

Length: 20 cm (8 inches)   **Family:** Woodpeckers

Of the five species of woodpecker (also known as Carpenter Birds) which are found in Trinidad, three, including this one, are also found in Tobago. They are widespread in woodland, where some birds prefer large dead trees. The smaller species are frequently seen amidst lower vegetation; they climb spirally up a trunk, reach the top, fly off to another tree and repeat the process.

This species is golden-olive above and finely barred dark and yellow below. It has a distinctively marked head: the nape and (in the male) the moustachial streak are red, the forehead is dark blue and the rest of the face is yellowish white. The single piercing call-note, *keek*, is often uttered.

Golden-olive Woodpecker

Red-crowned Woodpecker

Orange-winged Parrot

Its food consists largely of beetle larvae, but it will also take berries and is sometimes suspected of damaging cocoa pods. It nests in tree-holes, and both parents share nesting duties. 'Drumming', which is a form of breeding display, is short and less noticeable in this species than in others.

◆ Red-crowned Woodpecker   *Melanerpes rubricapillus*

Length: 17 cm (7 inches)   **Family:** Woodpeckers

This is one of the few common birds of Tobago that is not found in Trinidad. On the smaller island it is mainly found at lower levels amidst open country with a variety of trees, including coconut palms. It seems quite at home in suburban areas and gardens. The upper-parts and wings are barred black and white, with a white rump that shows prominently in flight; the underparts are olive brown, while the crown and nape are more or less red, especially in male birds. The call-notes include a loud, rattling trill, often repeated.

This noisy and very sociable species lives mainly on insects, dug out of crevices, but also takes berries and is known to feed on sugar water at feeding tables. It drums loudly during the breeding season, often gaining extra noise from drumming on galvanised roofs. Both parents share nesting duties, often making their nest in dead coconut palms or even telephone poles.

◆ Orange-winged Parrot   *Amazona amazonica*

Length: 32 cm (13 inches)   **Family:** Parrots

This species is so widespread in parts of both islands that occasionally it reaches pest proportions. In Trinidad it is frequently found in lowland areas, especially swampy forests, but it also inhabits parts of the Northern Range. In Tobago it is mainly confined to the lighter areas of forest and cultivated land. The most common Amazon parrot on our islands, it can be recognised by its size and by its plumage, which is green with orange in both the wings and tail. The forehead and lores are blue, and there is some yellow on the crown and cheeks. The call is an inimitable scream, often heard in chorus. Although it sometimes occurs in sizeable flocks, more commonly it is seen flying high overhead, often in pairs.

Feeding on fruits, seeds and flowers, this parrot can cause con-siderable damage to cocoa cultivation. It nests in holes, often in a palm tree. It is often kept as a pet, but it is not known as a great talker, as are some other species.

◆ Squirrel Cuckoo — *Piaya cayana*

Length: 42 cm (17 inches) **Family:** Cuckoos

This large and beautiful cuckoo is called by some of the older folk in Trinidad by the name 'Coucou manioc'. Living in forests and the adjoining cultivated lands with large trees, it moves about swiftly and elegantly, gliding on short flights from tree to tree or leaping with fluid, squirrel-like agility among the branches. Its long, barred tail is used for balance when landing. Generally it is rufous brown in colour, being paler below; the bill is yellow. The commonest call is a sharp, high-pitched *kik*, but it also utters a variety of other grating notes.

Squirrel Cuckoo

This species feeds mainly on large insects, such as grasshoppers, cockroaches and cicadas, seizing these as it darts about among the upper branches. It is not a parasitic species, but nests in a rather loose cup of vegetation, laying two white eggs; both parents share the duties of incubation and care of the young.

◆ Blue-crowned Motmot   *Momotus momota*

Length: 45 cm (18 inches)   **Family:** Motmots

This extraordinary bird is known locally as 'King of the Woods'. It is notable as the only species from our islands to have a racquet-tipped tail; the barbs close to the tips of the long central tail feathers fall out soon after maturity. Its strikingly beautiful plumage consists of green upperparts, a black crown which is encircled with turquoise, reddish underparts and a blue tail. The strong bill is black. Motmots sometimes inhabit forest undergrowth where they lurk in the deep shadow. In Tobago, however, they are often seen in

Blue-crowned
Motmot

cultivated areas, or perched on wires and branches beside road banks. The call is a deep, muffled hoot, often heard in the early morning or at dusk.

Motmots feed on a variety of invertebrates, but they also take fruit, small reptiles or sometimes even fledglings, and can be tamed to come for scraps. They nest in long tunnels which are dug into banks, where they are soft enough. White eggs are laid at the end of the tunnel, but no nest is made.

◆ Rufous-tailed Jacamar *Galbula ruficauda*

Length: 25 cm (10 inches) **Family:** Jacamars

This brilliant and excitable bird superficially resembles a very large hummingbird, but it is actually more closely related to the motmots. Found amidst cultivated areas or in light woodland, it likes to perch in the open or on the edge of a clearing, from where it flies out at intervals to catch its insect prey. The upperparts are iridescent bronze-green and the underparts are mostly reddish. Males differ from females in that they have white, rather than buff, throats. Both tail and bill are long and slim. The call is a high-pitched, rising series of notes, *pee-pee-pee*, etc.

The Jacamar catches large flying insects, such as butterflies and dragonflies, and strips their wings off before eating them at its perch. Often several jacamars, possibly related birds, may be found together at a favourite perching place. Like the motmots, the parent birds tunnel into soft banks to lay their eggs, but their nest-holes are considerably smaller.

◆ Streaked Flycatcher *Myiodynastes maculatus*

Length: 22 cm (9 inches) **Family:** Tyrant Flycatchers

This species is a fairly common member of the very large neotropical family of Tyrant Flycatchers, the great majority of which are cryptically coloured in brown and easily confused. The Streaked Flycatcher resembles others too, but is unlikely to be confused in our islands, since it is the only fairly large flycatcher heavily streaked, with a heavy bill and a conspicuously reddish tail. It is also a very noisy, conspicuous bird that relies on its aggressive nature for defence. Frequenting forest edges and cultivated lands with tall trees, it sometimes ventures into suburban areas. The call-notes are an excited series of harsh notes, *chip-chip* or *chipper-chipper*.

Rufous-tailed Jacamar ♂

Streaked Flycatcher

Although a flycatcher, it habitually prefers larger insects, such as beetles and locusts, and is known to take even small lizards. It nests in tree-holes or cavities, with an open cup of leaves or twigs, in which it lays up to three spotted eggs. Like the Kiskadee, its aggressive nature serves to protect its nest and young.

◆ Crested Oropendola   *Psarocolius decumanus*

Length: male 42 cm (17 inches)   **Family:** Orioles and Blackbirds
female 32 cm (13 inches)

This extraordinary species, commonly called 'Yellowtail' or 'Cornbird', is widespread on both islands at forest edges and in cultivated areas with large trees. Generally black with a chestnut brown rump, it has a long tail which is mostly bright yellow, a long and powerful whitish bill and bright blue eyes. The thin crest is often not visible. The call is variable, but consists mostly of loud, hoarse, gurgling notes, intermingled with clucks and unmusical trills. It is often accompanied by wing flapping, feather rustling, and a noise like that of tearing paper.

Crested Oropendola

Gregarious and polygamous, Yellowtails nest in colonies of up to 50. The metre-long, stocking-shaped nests are made of strips of vegetation which are woven together by the female and attached to the branches of a tall tree. Each colony has one dominant male and several subordinate males, all of whom share the females who look after the incubation and the care of the young. Though fairly omnivorous, and inveterate nest robbers, Yellowtails feed frequently on corn, citrus and cocoa, and so are considered to be agricultural pests.

◆ Lineated Woodpecker   *Dryocopus lineatus*

Length: 33 cm (13 inches)   **Family:** Woodpeckers

Lineated Woodpecker

One of the two larger woodpeckers to be found on Trinidad, and the more widespread, this species attracts attention by its loud, ringing call and by its energetic drumming. Generally black above, bordered by a whitish stripe from cheek to flank, and barred black and buff below, its most noticeable feature is the spectacular red crest extending to the nape. The male also has a scarlet patch on the face below the white stripe. These woodpeckers frequent the larger trees, often quite high up, where they explore dead wood and crevices looking for beetles and other insects.

This woodpecker is often found on *Cecropia* trees, searching for the pupae of the ants that live on the tree. It can often be heard pecking into the tree, as it looks for food, but this should not be confused with its drumming, which is a territorial signal to other birds. It nests in tree-holes, often in a large tree up to 20 metres above ground.

4 The Forest

◆ Rufous-breasted Hermit

Glaucis hirsuta

Length: 12 cm (5 inches)

Family: Hummingbirds

One of the larger members of its family, this hummingbird is common on both islands. It prefers the shaded undergrowth in forests and cultivated land and is often found along the beds of mountain streams. Hermit hummingbirds differ from most other hummingbirds by their duller, less iridescent plumage. Mostly brown in colour, this species is most easily distinguished by its long, decurved bill, its yellow lower mandible, and the prominent white tips to its rufous tail feathers. It is difficult to distinguish the male from the female.

Rufous-breasted Hermit

It feeds largely on nectar from a variety of forest plants, but also takes small spiders and insects. The nest is a flimsy hammock of rootlets. It is attached by a spider's web to the underside of a fern or similarly shaped leaf, often overhanging a bank or stream-bed.

Two other Hermit species are found in Trinidad. The males of these species form leks (or display areas), low down amidst forest vegetation. They sing monotonously and perform certain stylised movements for long periods every day throughout most of the year.

◆ White-tailed Sabrewing — *Campylopterus ensipennis*

Length: 13 cm (5 inches) **Family:** Hummingbirds

This remarkable hummingbird has gradually recovered from near extinction on Tobago following extensive hurricane damage to the hill forests in 1963. Still uncommon, it can now be found regularly in parts of the Main Ridge forest. Mainly green, with a violet-blue throat, its predominant feature is the largely white outer tail, which is conspicuous in flight; the bill is decurved and fairly long. Male birds sing persistently with a loud single note, *crreeet*, remaining at

White-tailed Sabrewing

the song perch for much of the day during the breeding season. The female is a bit duller, especially on the underparts.

This fairly large hummer feeds at forest plants, especially bromeliads, and also takes flying insects. Its nest is rarely found, but is quite substantial – a cup of moss and narrow leaves and rootlets. As with all hummers, only the female incubates and feeds the young.

The threat to this species and its subsequent recovery has received much attention from conservationists and those interested in Tobago's wildlife, providing a good example of how such interest can be effectively harnessed in a good cause.

◆ Tufted Coquette   *Lophornis ornata*

Length: 7 cm (2 ¾ inches)   **Family:** Hummingbirds

The smallest hummingbird species in Trinidad is also possibly the most spectacular in the plumage of the male, for the green and reddish brown plumage is enhanced by an extraordinary chestnut crest and long trailing tufts, reddish with green spots, at the sides of the head, along with a golden-green throat. As usual, the female, who

Tufted Coquette ♂

needs camouflage at the nest, is dressed more soberly being green above and reddish below, with a noticeable pale bar across the rump.

In flight, this bird resembles a large bee, as it moves smoothly and deliberately from plant to plant to feed on the nectar. It is not common, but may be found mainly in various parts of the Northern Range forests.

◆ White-chested Emerald　　*Amazilia chionopectus*

Length: 10 cm (4 inches)　　　　　　**Family:** Hummingbirds

This hummingbird is one of the commoner species to be found in the Northern Range of Trinidad, but it is not known on Tobago. The sexes are similar, being brilliant green with some bronze gloss on the back, but largely white below. It is one of the most aggressive species, resolutely defending its feeding territory. Although many people suppose that hummers do not sing, this species shows that they do, even if the song is merely a squeaky chatter, repeated persistently from its favourite perch.

This hummer feeds on nectar from the flowers of many trees, including the showy Mountain Immortelle (*Erythrina*) whose orange blossoms are such a feature of the valleys of the Northern Range between November and February. It also feeds at smaller trees and many other herbaceous plants such as *Heliconia* and *Pachystachys*. Breeding occurs in the early months of the year, when it builds its small cup nest, situated usually quite near ground level.

◆ Trinidad Piping-Guan　　　　*Pipile pipile*

Length: 61 cm (24 inches)　　　**Family:** Guans and Chachalacas

This very rare bird, locally called 'Pawi', may be the islands' only endemic species. It is now confined probably only to remote parts of the Northern Range forests, although a few birds have been seen regularly for some years near Grande Rivière. Resembling a turkey, it is generally blackish brown with crest and wing coverts tipped white, and a long tail; eye-ring and bare skin around the bill are blue, wattles also blue and long red legs. The call is a whining series of whistles, and in display the wings make a loud rattle like a window blind. In recent years the authorities in Trinidad have tried to influence local people to protect this important species, but the numbers are still very low.

White-chested Emerald

Trinidad Piping-Guan

The Pawi feeds on a variety of small fruits, taken from forest trees. It tends to move around, like most guans, in small groups, but very little is known about its way of life. No nest has yet been found, but most other guans build a platform of sticks, often placed fairly low in a tree.

◆ Rufous-vented Chachalaca　　*Ortalis ruficauda*

Length: 55 cm (22 inches)　　　**Family:** Guans and Chachalacas

More commonly known as 'Cocrico', this turkey-like bird was chosen as the national bird of Tobago, and so it adorns the country's coat of arms. It is not found in Trinidad. It mainly frequents Tobago's hill forest, but since the 1963 hurricane has become widespread also in the secondary growth adjoining cultivated land, where farmers claim it damages some crops. With the abandonment of many farms it has become quite numerous. Normally remaining in thick undergrowth, the Chachalaca keeps in contact with other members of its group by an extremely loud and raucous call, which has given it the common name.

Rufous-vented Chachalaca

This species also feeds largely on berries, small fruits and the young shoots of a variety of plants. It is also fond of dust bathing, in the manner of domestic poultry. It makes a rather flimsy nest of sticks and leaves, placed in a forest tree, laying up to four pale yellow eggs. Soon after hatching, the young leave the nest and follow their parents around for food and protection. Unfortunately, its choice as national bird has not brought it much protection, as many people like to eat it.

◆ Scaled Pigeon — *Columba speciosa*

Length: 30 cm (12 inches)   **Family:** Pigeons and Doves

This large pigeon is the only one seen commonly over the forests of the Northern Range in Trinidad. It is not known on Tobago, where its place is taken by a closely related species, the Pale-vented Pigeon (*Columba cayennensis*). Both species are well known to hunters as 'Ramier'. The Scaled Pigeon is generally dark brownish purple, edged with white, giving a scaled effect; the bill is bright red tipped white. It never seems to feed low in the forest, preferring the tree-tops where it feeds on a variety of fruits, especially the hog-plum (*Spondias*).

Scaled Pigeon

This species is usually seen singly or in small groups, flying high above the forest or perched in tree-tops. Its call is a deep cooing in two or four syllables. The nest of sticks is placed high in a forest tree, but little is known about the species, since it is so extensively hunted and is very wary of humans.

◆ Collared Trogon   *Trogon collaris*

Length: 25 cm (10 inches)   **Family:** Trogons

One of the most beautiful birds to be found in our islands, this species is fairly widespread in the forests and second growth, where it is found in the branches of forest trees below the canopy, only occasionally at lower levels. The male is mainly green above with black wings edged white; below it has a white breast-band above brilliant scarlet underparts; as so often, the female is less spectacular, being brown above and paler red below. Trogons tend to sit

Collared
Trogon ♂

motionless on a branch, where they are often hard to locate, but the call, a soft series of plaintive whistles, helps a patient observer to find the bird.

Trogons feed on small fruits, which they pluck from a tree, but also on insects and spiders, which are taken when the bird swoops suddenly from its perch. They nest in tree-holes or often in large termite nests, which they excavate before laying two white eggs; both adults attend the nest and feed the young.

◆ Channel-billed Toucan *Ramphastos vitellinus*

Length: 51 cm (20 inches) **Family:** Toucans

This is the sole member of this well-known family to be found in Trinidad, but it does not occur in Tobago. It is well distributed throughout forests, but it is often not noticed because it keeps largely to tree-tops and rarely descends to near the ground. Generally black in colour, the Toucan is bright red on the breast and above and below the tail; the throat and the sides of the neck are white and bordered below with orange. At the base of the great bill is a light blue bare patch around the eye. The call is a high-pitched, repeated, single note and sounds rather like a yelping dog.

Channel-billed Toucan

Bearded Bellbird ♂

Great Antshrike ♂

The Toucan feeds mostly on wild fruit but is also known to steal nestlings from other birds, and to eat insects. It hops about dexterously among the upper branches, sometimes in small groups, and flies with long swoops. It nests in a tree-hole, which is often an abandoned woodpecker's hole and is usually high in a tree.

◆ Bearded Bellbird   *Procnias averano*

Length: 28 cm (11 inches)   **Family:** Cotingas

This rather bizarre species inhabits deep forests in Trinidad. It is often very difficult to see, owing to its habit of perching fairly high up among the branches. It is also quite shy. Occasionally a male will call from a bare branch above the canopy, but more often calls from below the tree-tops. The male is unmistakable, being white with a brown head and black wings, and having many black wattles, resembling pieces of string, hanging from his throat. Females and immatures are olive-green above and yellowish streaked with green below. The strong bill is rather short and hooked at the tip. Males call an extremely loud *bock*, resembling the striking of an anvil, or a regular series of more musical notes, sounding a little like a bell (hence the local name, 'Campanero').

Bellbirds feed on highly nutritious fruit and resemble manakins in their breeding habits. Females perform all nesting duties, while adult males gather in small groups at a lek, where each male calls and displays on specially chosen branches at mid-level in a forest tree. Here he calls and jumps about between the branches, displaying his extraordinary plumage and hoping to attract a female, while discouraging rival males.

◆ Great Antshrike   *Taraba major*

Length: 20 cm (8 inches)   **Family:** Antbirds

This species is common in cultivated lands and forest edges in Trinidad, where it is found inhabiting thick undergrowth and rarely emerging into the open. The male is mainly black above with white wing bars and all white underparts; the bill is strong and hooked at the tip, while the eyes are red. As in many species of antbird, the female resembles the male, except that the black parts of the plumage are replaced by reddish brown. Since these birds move about within thick vegetation, they communicate by frequent calls; there are two main song sequences, both rattling series of notes, one accelerating and the other getting slower! This species is hard to see, but is not shy, so a persistent observer will succeed.

Antbirds mainly feed on invertebrates of many kinds; this species takes large insects but is also known to take small lizards as well as seeds. It nests in a well-made hammock made of roots and grass, slung fairly low in a bush or small tree. Both adults share nesting duties, which last for about one month.

◆ Black-faced Ant-thrush   *Formicarius analis*

Length: 20 cm (8 inches)   **Family:** Ground Antbirds

This interesting species differs from other antbirds in that it is almost entirely terrestrial, being found in forests and second growth in Trinidad, usually walking busily about on the forest floor in search of its prey. The sexes are similar and generally resemble small chickens with an upturned tail; the plumage is largely dark brown, with black face and throat and a conspicuous white eye-ring; legs are comparatively long. The species is fairly confiding and will only fly as a last resort, preferring to walk quietly away if disturbed. The call is memorable and easily imitated, which can sometimes attract a closer approach by the bird; it is a series of sev-

Black-faced Ant-thrush

eral sharp whistles, given in a repeated sequence, usually descending in pitch.

Like many antbirds, this species is attracted by the presence of a column of army ants, which cause most other insects and small creatures to attempt to escape. The birds exploit this situation, since their prey is thus easier to locate and capture. Sometimes an army ant column will attract a dozen or more antbirds or woodcreepers, as they wait nearby for their victims to show themselves. This species nests in hollow tree-stumps, but nests are rarely found and the life history of the species is not well known.

◆ Golden-headed Manakin   *Pipra erythrocephala*

Length: 9 cm (3 ½ inches)   **Family:** Manakins

The two members of this family found in Trinidad are some of the island's most interesting local birds. This species usually inhabits deep forests, chiefly in the Northern Range, but is also found in cultivated areas and secondary scrub. The male is almost all black but

Golden-headed Manakin ♂

has a bright golden head and white thighs, edged with a red band; his legs are pinkish and uniquely the iris of the eyes is white. The inconspicuous female is olive-green all over. The calls consist of a variety of sharp buzzing trills and shrill whistles, often associated directly with display, when the males make different explosive sounds in the course of their stereotyped movements, accompanying their flights and postures with loud squeaks, buzzes and rattles.

Manakins feed largely on small berries, which are readily available year-round. This enables the males to develop complex mating rituals, in this case at leks, where they congregate through the year displaying to each other and to visiting females. Each group of about six males gathers at a horizontal branch below the forest canopy, where they compete among each other by stereotyped flights and other movements, including certain postures. Often the males perch in a line along the branch, changing places as each one flies out and back, and adopting poses, often with one leg held out sideways displaying the red 'garter'.

◆ Blue-backed Manakin — *Chiroxiphia pareola*

Length: 14 cm (5 $\frac{1}{2}$ inches) **Family:** Manakins

Blue-backed Manakin ♂

On Tobago there is only one manakin species, but it is one of the island's most remarkable birds. Living mainly in thick forest, but also found in second growth, it frequents mid-levels in the trees, but occasionally descends nearer the ground, looking for the small fruits on which it feeds. The male is largely black with a V-shaped scarlet crest and sky-blue back. Again, the female is inconspicuous green all over. The call-notes are quite complex, including a sharp *weet*, along with a repeated chirping note, usually given by two males synchronously, which serves to 'invite' males to the display area. This is a specially chosen horizontal branch, often quite near the ground, where the males perform their joint display.

Since female manakins perform all nesting duties, the males are free to concentrate on their display rituals. In this species at least two, sometimes three, males perch on the chosen branch, then alternately each bird jumps up a metre or less, to land again on the perch, uttering a strange buzzing cry. This performance may continue for a minute or more, usually increasing in tempo until the birds seem to be leaping over each other in a circular motion. If a female is watching this display, she may be stimulated to invite the chosen male to mate.

◆ Rufous-breasted Wren   *Thryothorus rutilus*

Length: 12 cm (5 inches)   **Family:** Wrens

Rufous-breasted Wren

Though less well known than the House Wren, this engaging little bird is probably just as common. It inhabits light woodland, undergrowth and dense thickets in forest. It rarely ventures out into the open, but skulks in low bushes or forages in vines and lianas. However, it is not particularly wary of humans. It is greyish brown above, with a barred tail and a conspicuously speckled black and white throat; the breast is reddish and the lower underparts brown. These birds frequently associate in pairs, calling to each other amidst the undergrowth in a 'duet' of alternating similar phrases; these are loud musical whistles, usually ending in a flourish.

It feeds on small insects which are taken from the ground or from vegetation. The nest is a fairly large ball of leaves or grass with a wide side entrance, and is usually situated amidst a tangle of low vegetation. Both parents attend to the young. Both wrens are heavily parasitised at the nest by the Shiny Cowbird.

◆ Green Honeycreeper *Chlorophanes spiza*

Length: 14 cm (5 $\frac{1}{2}$ inches) **Family:** Tanagers

Green Honeycreeper ♂

Honeycreepers are small members of the tanager family, almost all brightly coloured. They move quickly through the upper branches of forest trees in search of nectar and small fruits, supplemented sometimes by some insects. This species is quite common in the Northern Range of Trinidad, where it is found mainly in the canopy of large forest trees. The male is a bright metallic green, tinged with blue, and has a black cap which contrasts sharply with his yellow beak. The female is similar, but paler green and lacks the black cap. Their call is an incisive *chip*, rather similar to that of several other species.

The Green Honeycreeper plucks small fruits from the trees, but also frequently takes nectar from blossoms of the large flowers of the Mountain Immortelle tree. Its nest, which is not often found, is a small cup of leaves and rootlets. The eggs are white with brown spots, like those of all other honeycreepers.

◆ Purple Honeycreeper *Cyanerpes caeruleus*

Length: 11 cm (4½ inches) **Family:** Tanagers

This attractive little tanager is common in the forests of Trinidad's Northern Range, but it is not very well known, since it feeds and

Purple Honeycreeper ♂

moves about mainly in the canopy. However, it readily comes to bird feeders in its area, so can usually be found at the Asa Wright Nature Centre. The adult male is a beautiful violet-blue with some black on head and wings, and has startlingly bright yellow legs; the female is less conspicuous but is equally colourful, being green with reddish and blue streaks on the face and throat; the bill is thin and decurved, and is used especially for extracting nectar from blossoms. Birds with conspicuous plumage rarely have noteworthy songs, and this little bird merely utters a thin, light *tsip*.

Feeding on fruits as well as flowers, these birds tend to move around in loose flocks, possibly based on family connections. Thus they can usually be located at trees that are in full flower or with ripe fruit. Little is known of their nesting, except that the nest is a small cup of moss lined with rootlets. Both parents assist in the care of the young.

◆ Red-legged Honeycreeper   *Cyanerpes cyaneus*

Length: 13 cm (5 inches)   **Family:** Tanagers

Like its congener, this spectacular little bird is one of the most colourful species to be found in Trinidad and Tobago. It is a true

Red-legged Honeycreeper ♂

forest bird and is most commonly found feeding among the higher branches of forest trees, often in the emergent twigs and leaves. It also feeds commonly at the red flowers of the *Norantea* vine. The male is largely dark violet-blue and black, but has a turquoise crown and pale yellow on the underwing and inner flight feathers, which only show up in flight. In contrast with its close relative, the male has bright red legs. After moulting, the male resembles the dull green female, except that he has black wings and tail, before changing back into breeding plumage for the next season. The bill is quite fine and slightly decurved.

The nest is a flimsy cup of grass and roots or moss, set at medium height in a forest tree, where the female carries out most of the care of eggs and young. The adult birds often form small (maybe family) groups of about half a dozen birds that forage and perch together in the tree-tops, but like many species with such habits they are hard to study.

◆ Violaceous Euphonia   *Euphonia violacea*

Length: 11 cm (4½ inches)   **Family:** Tanagers

Commonly known as 'Semp', this little tanager is well known in Trinidad where it is frequently kept in captivity as a pet. It is abun-

Violaceous Euphonia ♂

dant in forests and second growth, including cultivated land, provided there are some large trees. The male is a handsome bird, glossy blue-black above with a little white on wings and tail; the underparts and a small patch in front of the crown are bright golden-yellow. The female and immatures are olive-green above and yellowish olive below. The call is extremely musical and varied, with many different notes and squeaks. It often mimics other bird species, especially thrushes.

The Semp feeds principally on small fruits and berries, especially those of mistletoe and other epiphytes. The nest is a sphere of leaves and moss with a side entrance; it is often situated on the ground at the top of a bank, but cavities are also used. The three or four eggs are white marked with red. Both parents share the duties of feeding the young.

◆ Bay-headed Tanager   *Tangara gyrola*

Length: 14 cm (5 $\frac{1}{2}$ inches)   **Family:** Tanagers

This is the most common of the three medium-sized forest tanagers known in Trinidad; none of these is found in Tobago. It is often seen in forest or secondary growth at all altitudes, but is particularly common in the Northern Range. The male and female are similar in appearance: generally green with a reddish brown head; in fresh plumage some individuals show a golden tinge on the back. Immature birds lack the red head. Like the other forest tanagers, the call is a single metallic note or a light twittering.

It feeds mainly on small fruits from a variety of forest trees, vines and epiphytes. It also forages in small groups for insects among the foliage at all levels. The nest is a neat cup made mostly of moss and set in the fork of a small tree; the clutch of two eggs are white with brown markings. Up to three broods may be reared in one season, each taking about one month to produce.

◆ Turquoise Tanager   *Tangara mexicana*

Length: 14 cm (5 $\frac{1}{2}$ inches)   **Family:** Tanagers

Similar in many ways to the Bay-headed Tanager, this lovely little tanager is a gem. Mainly black above with blue face, breast and rump, and yellow underparts, it has a brilliant turquoise patch on the wing coverts. The sexes are similar. Found in a wide variety of habitats in Trinidad, including forests, cultivation and second growth,

Bay-headed Tanager

Turquoise Tanager

it even occurs in suburban gardens, moving swiftly about in small groups of about half a dozen; it is rarely seen on its own. The call is barely distinguishable from that of other members of the genus.

Feeding at all levels from the ground to the canopy, this tanager takes small fruits of many kinds, and also forages among thin twigs for insects. Its breeding habits are unusual, for several adults may take part in the rearing of the young in the nest, as if the family relationship is so strong that the individuals share breeding responsibilities among more than just the usual pair.

◆ Speckled Tanager   *Tangara guttata*

Length: 14 cm (5 $\frac{1}{2}$ inches)   **Family:** Tanagers

The third member of this genus of tanager found in Trinidad is perhaps the most spectacular of all, with its generally green or blue plumage set off by yellow tinges and black centres to many feathers. It is also the least widespread, being confined largely to the higher parts of the Northern Range, where it inhabits an almost sub-tropical zone of rain forest. Like the others it relies on keeping together in small groups, with its weak chirping calls clearly of less importance for its survival than its brilliant plumage. It lives on

Speckled Tanager

small berries and fruits, but supplements this diet with some invertebrates. The birds may be seen moving around among the higher branches of forest trees, searching the branches and twigs for prey, often gleaning them underneath the leaves.

Few nests of this species have been found in Trinidad. They are small cup-shaped structures, made of leaves, roots and fungal hyphae. Two spotted eggs are laid, which are incubated by the female alone; the male assists in feeding the young. It is believed that the adults stay together throughout the year.

5 Swamps, Marshes and Reservoirs

◆ **Anhinga**   *Anhinga anhinga*

Length: 86 cm (34 inches)   **Family:** Anhingas or Darters

Known by a variety of local names, including 'Snake-bird', this unique water-bird prefers freshwater habitats, including lakes and reservoirs, especially where they are bordered by trees and other vegetation, where it likes to perch. Resembling the cormorant to some extent, the Anhinga does not flock but hunts by itself under water, emerging to perch nearby, often being seen on a tree-stump with wings outstretched as if to dry them. Although mainly black, the male bird has striking white markings on its wings, while the female (and immature) has a brown head, neck and breast. The tail is long and broadly tipped buff. The dagger-shaped bill is ideally suited for its diet of fish.

When swimming under water, the Anhinga occasionally puts up its head and neck, which somewhat resembles a snake, and will often withdraw its head down without diving. When it catches a fish it will sometimes juggle it into position, so as to swallow it head first. The nest is a rough structure of sticks placed into a tree-fork. Previously anhingas departed from our islands to breed on the mainland, but recently have been breeding on both islands.

◆ **Cocoi Heron**   *Ardea cocoi*

Length: 112 cm (45 inches)   **Family:** Herons

Known to some (erroneously) as the 'Crane', this very large heron visits Trinidad and (rarely) Tobago during the dry season, preferring to breed in Venezuela later in the year. It resembles other large species (such as the Great Blue Heron, *Ardea herodias*) both in appearance and in its slow, stately manner of flight. It is generally

Anhinga

Cocoi Heron

grey, but has a white head, neck and breast, white thighs, and a black crown and flanks. The long bill is mostly yellow.

This heron stands motionless for long periods of time. It feeds, at the edge of a reservoir or in a marsh, by waiting patiently for an opportunity, then suddenly striking out at a fish or other aquatic creature. Unlike many other heron species, this one tends to be solitary. Unfortunately, its size attracts the attention of some hunters, so it is rather shy and avoids human contact.

◆ Snowy Egret · *Egretta thula*

Length: 57 cm (23 inches) · · · · · · · · · · · · · · · · **Family:** Herons

This beautiful heron is found on both islands in swamps and marshland, and along the coast where it feeds in shallow water. Some of these birds migrate to our islands during the North American winter, while others breed locally. Since it is all white, this species can be distinguished from other similar heron species only by its black

Snowy Egret

bill, yellow lores, and black legs with contrasting bright yellow toes. When they are in breeding plumage, the adults have beautiful, elongated plumes on the head and back (sometimes called aigrettes). Many years ago, these feathers were much in demand for the plume trade (now, thankfully, out of fashion).

Like other herons, this egret feeds largely on fish and other aquatic creatures. But instead of standing still and patiently waiting for their prey, Snowy Egrets dash about excitedly in shallow water, chasing their victims. Their nests are built low in mangrove trees, often in colonies with many nests together.

◆ Cattle Egret *Bubulcus ibis*

Length: 52 cm (21 inches)   **Family:** Herons

A comparative newcomer to the New World, the Cattle Egret probably arrived from Africa early in the twentieth century, and was first recorded in Trinidad in 1951. Since then the population has

Cattle Egret

rapidly expanded throughout the Americas, so that it is now the most numerous heron species on our islands. It is similar in appearance to the Snowy Egret, except that it is smaller and has a yellow bill and legs. In the breeding season, some of its feathers are tinged with a buff or orange hue, and the legs and bill become reddish.

Cattle Egrets feed mostly on grasshoppers and other insects found in pasture land. Since domestic animals that graze, such as cattle, disturb these insects as they move about, the egrets often wait beside them, seizing the insects as they move. Sometimes they even perch on the animal's back, which provides a good vantage point from which to spot their prey. Likewise, the birds often follow tractors. Cattle Egrets nest and roost in mangrove swamps, and they congregate at traditional sites (e.g. Caroni and Oropouche) every evening. Many flocks can be seen each evening moving to these roost-sites during the last hour of daylight.

◆ Yellow-crowned Night Heron
Nyctanassa violacea

Length: 64 cm (25 inches) **Family:** Herons

Frequently seen by day as well as at dusk, this medium-sized heron is a common resident of swamps and marshes on both islands, and

Yellow-crowned Night Heron

is also frequently found on the seashore, hunting mainly for crustaceans (hence its local name, 'Crabier'). The adult is an attractive bird, being mainly grey, but with a pattern of black and white markings on the head with a long crest; immature birds are brown with pale streaks. It is not normally gregarious, but at good feeding areas such as the coast at Waterloo many birds may be seen spread out over the mudflats.

The favourite prey of this heron is the fiddler crab, which lives in burrows in sand or mud. It also takes much larger crabs on rocky seashores, dismembering them and sometimes discarding the larger claws. The nest is a bulky platform of twigs, often situated quite high in a tree or coconut palm. Up to three light-blue eggs are laid and incubated by both parents.

◆ Scarlet Ibis *Eudocimus ruber*

Length: 57 cm (23 inches) **Family:** Ibises and Spoonbills

Scarlet Ibis

Undoubtedly Trinidad's most famous bird, the ibis was adopted in 1962 as the national bird; since then it has received official protection. Its numbers in Trinidad fluctuate because occasionally it is forced to migrate for safety to the Orinoco Delta in Venezuela. At their peak, the numbers in Caroni Swamp may reach 12 000. It is quite rare in Tobago, but occasionally large flocks visit for a time. The bright scarlet adult, with black wing tips and long curved bill, is unforgettable; but the mainly grey immature is much less spectacular.

The ibis roosts and nests in mangroves. It feeds over mudflats and in shallow swamp lagoons, probing the mud for small crabs, but also taking shrimps and small fish. It is a very gregarious species, feeding, flying, nesting and roosting in large flocks. Every evening, during the last hour of daylight, the flocks converge upon the roost-site in the Caroni Swamp (or, occasionally, at Oropouche or other mangrove swamps) creating a magnificent spectacle as they do so. The nest-sites are carefully guarded by the authorities, to prevent disturbance which might drive the colony to breed outside Trinidad.

◆ Black-bellied Whistling-Duck

Dendrocygna autumnalis

Length: 52 cm (21 inches)

Family: Ducks

Black-bellied
Whistling-Duck

There are three species of whistling-ducks, sometimes called tree-ducks, known on our islands; the Black-bellied is the largest and the most common. Whistling-ducks can be distinguished from other ducks by their longer necks and legs, their slower flight, and their habit of perching on trees or posts. This species is also notable for its bright red bill and conspicuous white wing patch which contrasts with its black flight feathers. Its high-pitched whistling call gives rise to its local name, 'Wi-chi-chi'.

Whistling-ducks are some of the few members of this family that breed locally. They nest at the height of the rainy season in marshy areas or rice fields, where they also feed. Unfortunately, this coincides with the hunting season, so the adults are unable to rear their families in peace. However, the Wildlife Trust at Pointe-à-Pierre has encouraged the recovery of the Black-bellied Whistling-Duck population by breeding some of these birds in captivity for subsequent release.

◆ **Masked Duck**　　　　　　*Nomonyx dominicus*

Length: 36 cm (14 inches)　　　　　　**Family:** Ducks

This small duck is not at all well known in our islands, partly because it is rare but also because of its highly secretive habits.

Masked Duck (a male and two females or young birds)

Living in freshwater marshes and remote pools, it spends its time amidst the thick vegetation such as water hyacinth (*Eichhornia*), where it feeds and may also nest. Accordingly, it is difficult to locate. When disturbed it dives or merely sinks beneath the surface, only flying as a last resort. The male is mainly rufous brown marked with some black, and with a white wing-patch only visible in flight; its bill is a startling pale blue; the female and immature are mainly brown with a buff head which has two horizontal black stripes. This species is sometimes known as a 'Stiff-tail' because of its fan-shaped tail which it sometimes holds erect, but it does not seem to have a local name, probably because of its rarity.

The nest of this species is placed amidst marshy vegetation or among rice plants. Again, because of its secretive lifestyle, little is known about its nesting details, but it may well have quite large clutches.

◆ Purple Gallinule   *Porphyrula martinica*

Length: 32 cm (13 inches)   **Family:** Rails

Often loosely referred to as a 'Water-hen', this marsh-dwelling species does indeed resemble a small domestic fowl. However, its brilliant

Purple Gallinule

dark blue plumage, with a bright red bill, below a pale blue shield, and white tail, sets it apart from a number of other species that may be found among the lilies and other vegetation of the typical fresh-water marsh in Trinidad or Tobago. It also has long yellow legs and extremely long toes which enable it to walk effectively on the marsh plants that float on the surface of the water. Seldom flying, and then only for short distances, this gallinule walks amidst the vegetation, searching for flowers, seeds and leaves of certain plants; occasionally it climbs into a low bush and, very rarely, it swims.

This gallinule utters a variety of clucks, squawks and fowl-like cackles, usually from thick cover, but rarely calls from the open except in alarm. Its nest is built amidst reeds or in a low bush, often mangrove or other swamp tree. Up to seven eggs, creamy spotted with dark brown, are laid; soon after hatching, the tiny, downy young leave the nest to follow their parents about. The immature plumage is dull brown with some bluish tinge, but the white tail is a good identification mark.

◆ Wattled Jacana

Jacana jacana

Length: 25 cm (10 inches)

Family: Jacanas

Wattled Jacana

Sometimes called 'Spurwing' or 'Lily-trotter', this marsh-dwelling bird is widespread in suitable habitats in Trinidad, but it is less common in Tobago. The Wattled Jacana prefers freshwater areas to brackish mangrove swamps; typically, it is found in small ponds with lilies covering the water and reed-beds around the edge. Mostly dark reddish brown, it shows conspicuous pale yellow wings when flying; the legs are quite long and the toes are enormous. Immature birds are whitish below with a prominent streak through the eye. This is a noisy species which calls with a high-pitched, rattling cry.

The Wattled Jacana feeds on aquatic creatures and makes its nest on a floating platform of lily leaves. The eggs are brown, beautifully patterned with black lines. The young are incubated and cared for by the male parent, who is abandoned by the female after she has laid the eggs. She then concentrates on searching for another mate, while the male parent cares for the eggs and the young when they hatch. He is a very solicitous parent, and can sometimes be seen to shelter the tiny young under his wings.

◆ Wilson's Plover   *Charadrius wilsonia*

Length: 19 cm (7 $\frac{1}{2}$ inches)   **Family:** Plover

Wilson's Plover

Nine species of plover have been recorded in our islands, and this is one of the less common ones. Most of them are migrants from North America, where they breed on the arctic tundra. Some winter in the West Indies, others merely pass through on their way to Argentina or Chile. This species is known to breed locally, usually on the muddy shores of the west coast of Trinidad. There are several similar species, each of which has a black breast-band on the white underparts, but this species has a longer, thicker bill than the others.

Although it associates with many other species of shorebird, it is usually not seen in flocks, but hunts individually, searching for crabs and other invertebrates on the mud. Plovers may be distinguished from most sandpipers by their common habit of running swiftly, stopping abruptly and then bending down to pick up food. Much time is spent standing motionless, often on one leg. When a nesting bird is disturbed, it may try to distract the intruder by feigning injury and calling with a plaintive whistle.

◆ Lesser Yellowlegs   *Tringa flavipes*

Length: 25 cm (10 inches)   **Family:** Sandpipers

Twenty-nine species from this family of shorebirds (or waders) have been recorded on our islands. Most of them are seen regularly,

Lesser Yellowlegs

either when they migrate from North to South America or when they spend the winter on the islands. With few exceptions, they leave to breed on the arctic tundra, but a few immature birds stay here over the mid-year. The Lesser Yellowlegs is one of the larger and more striking members of this family, with its long, straight bill, and long, slender, bright yellow legs. Many of the species in this family are distinguishable from the others by only slight differences. One distinguishing point is the voice. This bird's call is a light but plaintive *kew* or *kew-kew*.

It spends most of its time in flooded savannahs or rice fields, or on the edges of muddy pools in marshes, swamps or by the seashore; it feeds on fish, molluscs, worms and small crustaceans. It tends to be quite gregarious, forming flocks of 15–30 birds, and often associates with its smaller cousins. It has a noticeable habit of bobbing its head and tilting its body when alarmed.

◆ Black-necked Stilt   *Himantopus mexicanus*

Length: 36 cm (14½ inches)   **Family:** Stilts and Avocets

This beautiful wading bird is not uncommon in suitable habitat on Trinidad, but is rarely recorded in Tobago. It frequents mangrove swamps and marshes, also rice fields and the edge of the seashore. It is resident in Trinidad, but some individuals may migrate to the continent to breed. Outstanding because of its very long pink legs, it is conspicuous for its contrasting black and white plumage; the bill is quite long and thin. Often moving around in flocks, stilts are fairly excitable and utter a sharp, nasal *peent*, sometimes in chorus.

Stilts feed mostly on molluscs and aquatic insects obtained from the soft mud where they spend their days. They breed mostly in mangrove swamps, building a slight nest of roots and small sticks on the ground, relying on camouflage for protection. Up to four olive coloured eggs are laid, which are difficult to spot in such a situation. If disturbed at the nest, the parent bird will go through a distraction routine, calling and flapping its wings as if injured.

◆ Red-bellied Macaw   *Ara manilata*

Length: 51 cm (20 inches)   **Family:** Parrots

This is the only native macaw found on Trinidad, whose status can definitely be ascribed as natural, since other species (such as the Blue-and-Yellow Macaw) are so often imported or bought (and then

Black-necked Stilt

Red-bellied Macaw

released) that much confusion results as to their correct status. The Red-bellied, which does not occur on Tobago, is found amidst palm forests or freshwater swamps such as Nariva. It is a medium-sized macaw, mainly green with some blue above and red lower underparts. Like all macaws, it has a long tail and usually flies in small flocks or pairs. The call is a shrill scream, usually heard in chorus.

This macaw feeds on palm fruits, especially that of the Moriche (*Mauritia*), and is seldom found far from this typical habitat in eastern Trinidad. It nests in tree-holes, often in a dead palm, where up to three white eggs are laid. Fortunately for this macaw, it does not seem to attract the attention of trappers and pet fanciers as much as the more showy species, which are rapidly becoming scarce throughout their range. But the problem lies with the buyers, for impoverished peasants are tempted to break the laws for the high prices available, mostly from overseas buyers.

◆ American Pygmy Kingfisher   *Chloroceryle aenea*

Length: 14 cm (5 $\frac{1}{2}$ inches)   **Family:** Kingfishers

This is one of the two resident kingfishers on Trinidad; two other migratory species, both considerably larger, are sometimes seen

American Pygmy Kingfisher

also. All four species are found near water, especially in swampland, but also beside reservoirs and occasionally along the coast. This kingfisher is probably the least common, and it is very local in its distribution, being seen most commonly beside streams or pools adjoining mangroves, or even in the forest. The male is dark bluish green on the upperparts and head, with some small white spots on the wings; most of the underparts are chestnut brown with some white on the lower underparts. The female is similar, but the underparts are crossed by a green breast-band. The dagger-shaped bill is comparatively long and powerful.

Kingfishers feed on fish and aquatic insects, and they are usually seen flying rapidly and directly along a river, or perched quietly on an overhanging branch. The call of this species is a high-pitched squeak. The nest is made in a hole in a bank, and attended by both sexes.

◆ Yellow-chinned Spinetail *Certhiaxis cinnamomea*

Length: 15 cm (6 inches) **Family:** Ovenbirds

Members of this obscure family vary greatly in their habits and habitat. They are mainly small brown birds which easily escape

Yellow-chinned Spinetail

notice. But this species is a common inhabitant of freshwater marshes and swamp edges, which draws attention to itself by its shrill, rattling call and its comparative tameness. It is rich chestnut-brown above and white below, with a fairly long, graduated tail.

This spinetail feeds on small invertebrates which are found amidst low vegetation at the water's edge. It builds an enormous nest of twigs, which is placed near the ground, usually in a low bush or small tree. The nest is shaped like an oblong vessel with a 'spout' through which the bird enters. Up to three white eggs are laid in the nest-chamber. Often the nest is decorated with pieces of snakeskin or other bright objects. All three spinetail species in Trinidad may be parasitised by the Striped Cuckoo (see page 31), which removes the host's eggs and deposits its own. The mechanism of this exchange is not yet properly understood. The adult spinetails are very tame near their nests and will even sometimes repair them in the presence of human beings.

◆ Pied Water-Tyrant   *Fluvicola pica*

Length: 15 cm (6 inches)   **Family:** Tyrant Flycatchers

This dapper little bird is common in Trinidad in freshwater marshland or muddy savannahs, alongside reservoirs and the edges of

Pied Water-Tyrant

mangrove swamps. It is found near the ground or amidst low bushes. The sexes are similar in appearance: white, with black wings, upper back and tail. The call is a conspicuous, nasal, buzzing note, *zhweeoo*, which is repeated at irregular intervals.

This flycatcher feeds on small insects which are found at the water's edge and are sometimes caught in flight. It flits about actively, constantly bobbing up and down and is rarely seen in repose. The nest is a ball of dried grass, mixed with feathers or wild cotton, with the opening at one side. It is quite conspicuous, being constructed on a stump or low branch, almost always over water, where most predators cannot reach it. Both parents attend the nest, but, like other conspicuous nests, it is often visited by the parasitic Shiny Cowbird (see page 33).

◆ Yellow-hooded Blackbird *Agelaius icterocephalus*

Length: 18 cm (7 $\frac{1}{2}$ inches)   **Family:** Orioles and Blackbird

This species is a resident of freshwater marshland in Trinidad, where it is abundant. It frequents the edges of mangrove swamps and is also found in rice fields, flooded savannahs and along the edges of cane fields. The male is quite spectacular; he is glossy black with a brilliant yellow head, neck and upper breast, and black

Yellow-hooded Blackbird ♂

Red-capped Cardinal

Common Black Hawk

lores. The female is mainly brown with yellowish cheeks and throat. The male's call is a clucking note followed by a long-drawn-out wheezing note.

This highly gregarious species feeds on a mixture of seeds, especially rice, and a variety of invertebrates. It takes grain crops but also destroys many insect pests. Breeding is communal and the nest, a deep cup of grass stems, is slung amidst reeds or other water plants, sometimes in low trees. Many nests, sometimes in hundreds, are built together. The males are polygamous. The population is kept in check by heavy parasitism from the Shiny Cowbird, and these two species often flock together.

◆ Red-capped Cardinal *Paroaria gularis*

Length: 18 cm (7 inches) **Family:** Seedeaters

This attractive little bird is an uncommon resident of marshes and swamp edges in Trinidad, also beside reservoirs as at Pointe-à-Pierre. It can easily become quite tame and comes readily for scraps at picnic tables near Caroni Swamp. Mainly black above and white below, the adult has a scarlet head and throat patch, along with a black mask through the eye; immature birds have rather less red and are generally browner. The call is a sharp chirping. Rather a restless species, it moves quickly about in the low vegetation

This species feeds mainly on seeds, and will forage in long grass at the edges of savannahs. It nests in mangroves or other low trees, building a shallow cup nest of small twigs and stems, often fairly low in the tree. Two creamy eggs, spotted with brown, are laid. The adult birds often move about in pairs or small groups, and frequently perch in low trees or dart about quarrelling with other species.

◆ Common Black Hawk *Buteogallus anthracinus*

Length: 56 cm (22 inches) **Family:** Hawks

This large, powerful bird of prey is one of the commonest in its family on Trinidad, where it may be found both over forests and in more open country, usually near water or marshy areas, including mangroves. It is almost entirely black, but its tail has one broad white band and a white tip; the legs and base of the bill are yellow. Except for the white band it might be mistaken for a vulture, but the head, legs and bill are quite different. One good field-mark is the call, a high-pitched series of piping notes, usually uttered in flight. Sometimes two birds will circle together calling while high in the sky, and in a courtship movement attempt to grasp each other's talons while in flight.

This species seems to feed largely on crabs, which it finds among the rocks of the sea coast, in marshy pools or even in thick forest where a stream or river flows through. Often the remains of the crab shells are strewn about a feeding place, showing that the hawk has been there. It nests fairly high in a tree, laying usually just one pale blue egg. Young birds are streaked brown on the underparts, as are the young of many other hawks.

◆ Blue-and-yellow Macaw *Ara ararauna*

Length: 84 cm (33 inches)   **Family:** Parrots

This large and brilliantly coloured macaw has only recently been rescued from extinction on Trinidad. It existed in small numbers in the area of Nariva Swamp up until about 1970, when it succumbed to a combination of the destruction by a large fire in the roosting area and constant pressure by trappers and hunters. For about 40 years no wild macaws of this species were seen, although occasionally captive birds escaped or were released, including some on Tobago. Considerable efforts by conservation groups in recent years have led to the reintroduction of this species into its natural habitat in the Nariva area.

Wild individuals are largely restricted to wetter parts of the Nariva Swamp, especially where 'islands' of palm trees are found. This macaw is easily identified by its striking plumage, mainly bright blue upperparts and orange-yellow below. The very long tail is unmistakable, as is its deep, croaking call. This species usually moves about in small groups by day, looking for fruits and seeds of palms, especially Moriche Palms. There are only a few records of local birds breeding in the wild state, and clutches are small. The species tends to be solitary, but occasionally individuals are found in small groups at a roost together with flocks of the smaller Red-bellied Macaw.

6 The Coast

◆ Red-billed Tropicbird

Phaethon aethereus

Length: 100 cm (40 inches)   **Family:** Tropicbirds

The Red-billed Tropicbird is rarely seen off Trinidad. It is mainly found near the islands of Little Tobago and St Giles off the north-eastern coast of Tobago. Here it nests between December and April, but may usually be seen in the other months also. This beautiful seabird is mostly white, with some black on the back, head and wings. Its massive bill is bright red, and the two central tail feathers are elongated in the adult, extending for 50 cm (20 inches) and thus forming half the bird's total length. Its call is a shrill scream which is sometimes repeated in a long series.

Red-billed Tropicbird

Tropicbirds feed at sea by plunging from a height into clear water and taking fish from near the surface. They do not flock but are found in small groups at the breeding grounds. One speckled egg is laid on the ground, often on a cliff side or among rocks. While incubating or guarding the young, the parent is extremely tenacious, sometimes refusing to abandon the nest even when handled.

◆ Magnificent Frigatebird　　*Fregata magnificens*

Length: 100 cm (40 inches)　　　　　　**Family:** Frigatebird

Popularly known as the 'Man-o'-War Bird', the frigatebird is a familiar sight along the coasts of Trinidad and Tobago, gliding high above the sea or over the ridges of the Northern Range. In flight, it forms a distinctive silhouette in the shape of a shallow W, its long wings spread to their 2 metre (7 foot) wingspan. The long tail can occasionally be seen to be divided into a deep fork. The adult male is black all over, the female is black with a white breast, and the head and most of the underparts of the immature are white.

The frigatebird breeds on remote, undisturbed islands, such as St Giles off northeast Tobago. It nests in low trees and lays one white

Magnificent Frigatebird

egg. Both parents attend the nest, where the male often attracts his mate's attention by inflating his throat patch into a huge, scarlet 'balloon'. The diet is usually fish, but frigatebirds rarely fish for themselves, preferring to attack smaller seabirds, forcing them to disgorge their most recent meals, which the pirate then takes.

◆ Brown Pelican   *Pelecanus occidentalis*

Length: 120 cm (48 inches)   **Family:** Pelicans

This huge, heavy seabird with its long bill and enormous pouch is well known. The West Indian term 'Pillikin' refers not to this bird but to the much smaller terns. Pelicans are known all along the

Brown Pelican

coasts of both islands, and large flocks are often found in the Gulf of Paria and near Plymouth. Generally brown, the adult has a white crown and a band of chestnut on the back of the head; the wings have a silvery pattern.

Pelicans often swim in the sea or fly, usually in formation, in flocks of about a dozen. When it spots fish, the pelican dives down at a steep angle, folding its wings just before hitting the water. As it emerges, with a pouch full of small fish, gulls and terns often crowd around to steal the food out of the pouch! Pelicans nest in trees, but are often disturbed by poachers.

◆ Brown Booby   *Sula leucogaster*

Length: 75 cm (30 inches)   **Family:** Boobies

This seabird is common around the coasts of Tobago, but less common off Trinidad. Boobies keep further out to sea than gulls, terns and pelicans, flying low over the water and often gliding on their long, pointed wings. Adults are brown above and on the upper breast, and have white lower underparts; the stout, pointed bill is pale yellow, as are its feet. Immature birds are brown all over and their legs and bills are duller than those of the adults.

Although they usually hunt for food alone, boobies sometimes form loose flocks to exploit a rich food supply. They feed on small fish, diving below the surface, often quite deep, to catch them, even using their wings as underwater fins. They breed on rocky islands off Tobago, making a simple nest of flattened grass or vegetation on the ground and usually on a cliff side. One or two white eggs are laid, but it is rare for more than one chick to survive the long fledging period, so it seems as if the second egg is laid 'for insurance'.

◆ Laughing Gull   *Larus atricilla*

Length: 40 cm (16 inches)   **Family:** Gulls and Terns

This is the only seagull that is common in our area. It is found on the coasts of both islands and breeds on small islets off the Tobago coast. Many of these birds leave their breeding grounds between November and March, but during much of the year they are extremely common in their main feeding areas in the eastern Gulf of Paria between Caroni Swamp and San Fernando, and also near Scarborough or Plymouth in Tobago. During the breeding season, from April to August, adults develop a dark grey head; this becomes white in the 'off' season. The rest of the upperparts are grey, with

Brown Booby

Laughing Gull

black wing tips, and the underparts are white. Gulls fly with a slower wing action than the rather similar terns.

The Laughing Gull feeds on fish and other marine organisms, which it takes from the surface of the sea or along the shore, but it is also a scavenger for other food found on the coast. The nest is merely a depression on the ground. The young gulls are largely brown. Many of these seabirds like to rest on fishing boats, waiting for any signs of feeding action from other birds. If a shoal is found, all the birds soon leave to exploit the feast.

◆ Large-billed Tern　　　　　*Phaetusa simplex*

Length: 38 cm (15 inches)　　　　　**Family:** Gulls and Terns

This spectacular tern is a common visitor to Trinidad's west coast and adjoining marshes, where it feeds in the offshore waters, but is also found at reservoirs, ponds and rice fields. Its striking plumage shows a black head with dark back and primaries, offset by white wing coverts and secondaries and all white underparts; the massive bill is bright yellow. This is an inland river tern, only found at sea near the outflow of major rivers like the Orinoco, hence no authentic record yet from Tobago. It has a very loud call, resembling a goose, and often several birds join in a chorus.

This tern feeds like most others by surface plunging for small fish, but is also known to take flying insects. Although there are a

Large-billed Tern

few old breeding records from Trinidad, it is mostly absent during the breeding season, November to January, when it breeds on river islands in South American rivers. Although this species does not fly around in flocks, sizeable numbers may be seen resting together in the rice fields or on posts along the shoreline at Waterloo.

◆ Royal Tern   *Sterna maxima*

Length: 48 cm (19 inches)   **Family:** Gulls and Terns

The largest tern known from our islands, this magnificent seabird breeds and lives on the coast of both islands; also many others that breed in the north visit during the winter months. On Trinidad they may be found mostly on the sheltered west coast, likewise on Tobago they are more commonly found between Crown Point and Charlotteville, especially in the area of Plymouth and Buccoo. This is almost all white, with a black cap during the mid-year breeding period, and with a large, orange-red bill and black legs. Outside the breeding season adults lose most of the black on their crest. Breeding colonies are hard to locate, but they are probably on small offshore islets, such as the Sisters Rocks off Tobago.

Royal Tern

Roseate Tern (nesting colony)

Brown Noddy

The Royal Tern feeds on fish, for which it dives, and is therefore more commonly found in calm waters. They nest on the bare ground, usually laying only one egg. However, such eggs are very vulnerable to poachers and few successful colonies are found locally. On islands where protection is afforded, large colonies may develop involving hundreds of pairs.

◆ Roseate Tern   *Sterna dougallii*

Length: 38 cm (15 inches)   **Family:** Gulls and Terns

This beautiful and graceful seabird used to be considered just a visitor to our shores, but in recent years it has been found nesting, mainly on small rocky islets off Tobago, but also off the north coast of Trinidad. Almost all white, when in breeding plumage it sometimes has a rosy tinge to the breast, which certainly shows it off to advantage; the bill is mainly black during the 'off' season, but with a bright red base when breeding. This bird is usually found in flocks, both when feeding over the water and at the nesting grounds. The call is a rasping note, sometimes repeated in two syllables.

Like most other terns, Roseates feed by plunge diving, hunting small fish at the surface, especially when a shoal is being disturbed by larger fish beneath. At the nesting colony the birds nest on the bare ground, but they are very vulnerable to disturbance from humans, so nesting success can be disappointing. Often the adults can be seen resting on fishing boats at anchor just offshore.

◆ Brown Noddy   *Anous stolidus*

Length: 37 cm (15 inches)   **Family:** Gulls and Terns

Most tern species are largely white, but this tropical tern is distinguished by its dark brown plumage, with white forehead and wedge-shaped tail. It is widespread around Trinidad and Tobago and breeds on small islands offshore, if it is undisturbed by poachers, during the mid-year months. In the 'off' season they spend much time at sea, but many return at night to roost at their breeding grounds.

Noddies nest on cliff ledges or on rocky shores. The 'nest' is usually only a hollow but occasionally it is built of sticks. The young chicks are either dark grey or whitish; the dark type predominates in our areas. The adults feed at the surface of the sea and are often attracted by shoals of small fish being attacked by larger fish below, which cause the birds to gather in an excited flock to exploit the feast. Sometimes they settle on the water like gulls, but more often they are seen flying.

◆ Black Skimmer   *Rynchops niger*

Length: 45 cm (18 inches)   **Family:** Gulls and Terns

Although classified into this family, the Skimmer has a unique and extraordinary bill, the lower mandible being considerably larger than the upper. This species is mainly black above and white below; the base of the long bill is red, as are the short legs. Skimmers breed on mainland South America and visit Trinidad, especially the west and south coasts, mostly between May and November. Apart from the coasts, they also frequent marshes and reservoirs.

The Skimmer feeds by flying low over smooth water with the tip of the lower mandible skimming the surface. When it touches prey, the bill suddenly clamps shut. Since the birds also feed sometimes at night, it is thought that feeding birds may gain an advantage by retracing their path at the end of a feeding flight, when phosphorescent organisms disturbed on the previous attempt help the bird to find prey more easily. The birds often feed together in small flocks, and usually rest in flocks on mudbanks at the edge of the water.

Black Skimmer

7 The Air

◆ Black Vulture

Coragyps atratus

Length: 62 cm (25 inches)   **Family:** American Vultures

The 'Corbeau', as it is generally known, is probably the best known and least loved bird in Trinidad; oddly, it is seldom found in Tobago. It can be seen flying over all kinds of habitat and is particularly common at garbage dumps, along certain coasts (especially where fish offal is available), and in other places where carrion may be found. This species is more gregarious than the red-headed Turkey Vulture and it is often seen circling on thermal air currents in large numbers. At night they congregate in roosts, usually in large trees. The Black Vulture is all black with pale bases to the primaries, and can be distinguished from black hawks by its small head and, in flight, by its upturned wings.

Black Vulture

This vulture locates its food by sight (often noting the movements of other vultures), whereas the Turkey Vulture uses its highly developed sense of smell. In addition to carrion, the Black Vulture feeds on coconuts. It makes no nest, but merely lays its eggs at the base of a large tree in light woodland.

◆ Osprey   *Pandion haliaetus*

Length: 57 cm (23 inches)   **Family:** Hawks

Sometimes called the 'Fish Hawk', the Osprey visits our islands from its breeding ground in North America. During the northern winter it is fairly common along the coast and over swamps and reservoirs; a few immature birds remain between May and September. The long wings, with their 1.8 metre (6 foot) wingspan, bend noticeably, giving the bird a shallow W-shaped silhouette. The Osprey is mainly brown above and white below, and is one of the few hawks here with a white head, though it has a prominent black streak through the eye. The call is a series of piercing, mewing notes.

After flying high above the water, the Osprey dives feet first to catch its prey, so causing a mighty splash. The prey is usually fish, which may be up to 45 cm (18 inches) long. Its talons are immensely strong and roughly serrated to enable it to grip fish securely.

Osprey

Savanna Hawk

◆ Savanna Hawk   *Heterospizias meridionalis*

Length: 52 cm (21 inches)   **Family:** Hawks

This species is one which has benefited over the last half century from the expansion of cattle ranching in the eastern and central regions of Trinidad. It was formerly quite rare and localised, but may now be seen regularly at Waller Field and similar open savannah country. It is a large, long-legged hawk, generally reddish brown in colour with black wing tips and fine barring on the underparts. Its call is a loud scream which drops gradually in pitch.

Of all the local hawks, this one seems to be the most adaptable; it will eat almost any small animal, including rodents, snakes, lizards, frogs, crabs, fish and insects. Its usual method of hunting is to sit on a high perch, watch for its prey, and drop suddenly down on to it. The nest is usually built high among the leaves of a large palm or other tree overlooking the surrounding savannah.

Ornate Hawk-Eagle

◆ Ornate Hawk-Eagle   *Spizaetus ornatus*

Length: 61 cm (24 inches)   **Family:** Hawks

Probably the most spectacular of all the local resident raptors, this hawk-eagle is uncommon but ranges widely over Trinidad's Northern Range forests; there are a few records from Tobago. Largely dark brown above and white below, its nape, sides of head and breast are rufous, and the lower underparts and thighs are barred with black; it also has a long, pointed crest. Immature birds have white heads and are more generally white below. Most commonly this species is seen soaring high above the forest, calling a series of high-pitched, ringing notes in a repeated sequence.

Poultry farmers in the hills claim that this species steals their stock, but many such stories tend to be exaggerated. Nevertheless, this is a bird hawk, overpowering smaller birds with its size and strength. It also takes snakes. Nests are built high in a forest tree; they are bulky structures of many sticks and may be used year after year. There is usually only one young, which stays in or near the nest for several months before becoming independent.

◆ Merlin
Falco columbarius

Length: 30 cm (12 inches)   **Family:** Falcons

This fierce little raptor is a migrant to our shores during the northern winter, breeding in North America, so that it is only present on our islands between October and April. It is found mainly in open areas and savannahs, but may be seen hunting in suburban gardens and over forest on occasion. The male is dark grey above and paler below with heavy streaks; its tail is barred and it has yellow legs. Females and immature birds are similar, but brown above also.

This species is a bird hunter, though it also feeds on bats and small mammals. One of its principal prey species in Trinidad is a North American finch called the Dickcissel (*Spiza americana*), which often migrates in enormous numbers from the Midwest states of the United States and Canada, to spend the winter in Venezuela and Trinidad. Merlins may well accompany these huge flocks during the migration journey, preying on the finches at their roosting and feeding grounds here on the savannahs and in rice fields. The falcons also roam the shores of both our islands looking for shorebirds.

Merlin

◆ Gray-headed Kite

Leptodon cayanensis

Length: 48 cm (19 inches)   **Family:** Kites and Hawks

Like many birds of prey, this species is usually seen flying overhead in the forested parts of Trinidad. It is one of the larger kites, which can usually be distinguished by their languid manner of flight, often soaring in circles or gliding with the occasional lazy flap of the wings. The plumage is very varied, but the most commonly seen is generally dark above with a grey head, whitish underparts, barred under the rather broad wings, and a rather long, barred tail. Often the bird will perch in a forest tree, sometimes surprisingly low down, where it peers around looking for prey and occasionally calling its cat-like cry.

This kite feeds largely on insects and reptiles, like most others in the group, though it also takes frogs and even birds, especially the young and inexperienced individuals. Its nesting habits are not well known, like many other birds of prey, partly because the group is not very numerous. The nest probably resembles those of other kites, a rather flimsy collection of sticks, placed high in a tree. Both parents assist in nesting duties, though the female usually guards the young.

Gray-headed Kite

◆ Chestnut-collared Swift   *Streptoprocne rutila*

Length: 14 cm (5 ½ inches)   **Family:** Swifts

Superficially, swifts (sometimes known locally as rainbirds) resemble swallows, or even bats, but they can be distinguished by their long, tapering wings, which appear curved in flight, and by their streamlined bodies. This species, which is one of five rather similar swifts known on Trinidad, has wings which are much longer than its body. It is all black except for a ring of chestnut-brown all around its neck. It is slightly larger than the other species and is mainly confined to forested hilly areas.

Swifts perch only when they are at the nest or roost; they spend the rest of the time flying rapidly about hunting for small insects, which they take in flight with their wide-open mouths. Their nests are discs made of plant material, mixed with mud, which are attached to the rocky walls of caves or gorges in the mountains, usually near a stream. This nest may be used (after repair) for many years if the site is suitable. Two white eggs are laid, and the young fledge after a very long period of 40 days in the nest, being guarded by both parents. It is thought that many swifts fly continuously for many months after fledging, never landing but sleeping on the wing, until they too are old enough to breed.

Chestnut-collared Swift

Gray-breasted Martin

White-winged Swallow

◆ Gray-breasted Martin

Progne chalybea

Length: 17 cm (7 inches)   **Family:** Swallows

Although some local dispersal takes place, this large swallow is resident on Trinidad (and its outlying islands) throughout the year. A similar species, the Caribbean Martin (*Progne dominicensis*), inhabits Tobago between February and October. Adults are glossy blue-black on the upperparts, with greyish brown breast and flanks and white lower underparts. The tail is forked but not markedly. It is distinguished from other swallows by its more robust appearance, and by its habit of flying high for much of the time. The call is a single twangy note.

These martins feed by catching small insects in flight. They often congregate on wires in large numbers, especially in the evening. They like to feed or bathe at reservoirs, flying down to take insects or water from the surface. Nests are built in holes or crevices, which are often under house roofs and in cliff sides, but sometimes in pipes or on scaffolding. Both parents attend the nest.

◆ White-winged Swallow

Tachycineta albiventer

Length: 13 cm (5 $\frac{1}{2}$ inches)   **Family:** Swallows

This little swallow has been increasing in range recently on Trinidad, and has even found its way to Tobago. It lives in open areas, often near water such as at the seashore or around lakes and reservoirs, where it may be found perching on boats or other convenient spots like buoys or scaffolding. It is not a migrant nor does it associate with others in flocks. The adult bird is mainly dark blue or green above, with patches of white on the wings and rump, and white underparts; young birds have less or no white on the wing. Like most other swallows, its call is a sharp trill or double note.

This swallow feeds like others on small flying insects, taken in flight. It breeds during the mid-year, often using scaffolding or hollow pipes in which to make its nest of grass stems and feathers. Sometimes it may nest in broken stumps of bamboo. Up to six eggs are laid, but surprisingly little is known of its fledging period, even though it is fairly tolerant of humans and allows a close approach.

8 The Night

◆ Oilbird
Steatornis caripensis

Length: 45 cm (18 inches)

Family: Oilbirds

Locally called 'Guacharo' or 'Diablotin', this extraordinary bird is highly specialised in several ways. It spends the day in dark caves or gorges emerging at night to feed on fruit. Known locations in Trinidad include caves at the Asa Wright Nature Centre, Mount Aripo and the northern Oropouche river. All the habitats are remote and fairly inaccessible, being either in deep forest or on a rugged

Oilbird

sea coast. The adult bird, with its wingspan of over one metre, is rich brown in colour. It has a large, hooked bill and a long tail and so resembles both owls and nightjars in appearance.

Flying and feeding in near or total darkness, Oilbirds emit a series of clicks and the echoes from these enable them to navigate by sonar. This is the only nocturnal fruit-eating bird. It lives on the fruits of forest palms and certain other trees, which are located by smell. It breeds in caves, often underground, and nests on mounds which are built up of regurgitated remains of fruit. In the cold environment of the caves, eggs and young mature very slowly, so the breeding season is very long.

◆ Common Potoo   *Nyctibius griseus*

Length: 38 cm (15 inches)   **Family:** Potoos

Common Potoo

This very unusual species is a true night bird, that spends its days perched on a tree stump in the forest or among mangroves, where its amazing camouflage helps it to escape the notice of all but the sharpest observers. Related to the nightjars, potoos have long tails and cryptic brown or grey plumage that blends perfectly with the tree where it perches. Even when approached, the potoo usually stays still, with its eyes apparently closed, until the last moment before flying off. The call, given only at night, is an evocative, fairly loud series of five or six descending notes, that country folk used to think came from an anteater!

Potoos feed largely on moths and other large insects that they hunt in the air by night. They wait at a perch and fly up to seize the insect in flight. The 'nest' is merely a depression at a tree-fork, where the single egg is placed, sometimes several metres above ground. There is a long nesting period of over two months, with both parents taking turns to incubate or brood the young bird.

◆ Tropical Screech-Owl   *Otus choliba*

Length: 23 cm (9 inches)   **Family:** Owls

Tropical
Screech-Owl

This species is entirely nocturnal, although it may be disturbed occasionally from its daytime roost. It is a comparatively small owl, mainly grey or reddish brown, beautifully marked with black and white speckles above and with finely patterned markings below. Its short ear-tufts distinguish it from other local owls. It inhabits mainly light woodland and scrub on the edge of savannahs, but is also found on the forest edge. Pairs are often found together, and frequently a whole family with young in attendance may be encountered.

As with most nocturnal creatures, the calls are of extreme importance for contact as well as display. This owl calls a series of soft hoots, almost run together, and often ending with a single louder hoot. When disturbed the bird may react with various other noises, including wailing screams and angry caterwauling.

This species nests like most owls early in the year, building its nest inside a tree cavity or other convenient shelter. It lays up to three almost round white eggs, but usually no more than two young survive into adulthood. The food is largely insects and other invertebrates, but small bats are also taken, as well as other little mammals.

◆ Ferruginous Pygmy-Owl *Glaucidium brasilianum*

Length: 15 cm (6 inches)   **Family:** Owls

Ferruginous Pygmy-Owl

Known locally as 'Jumbie Bird', and associated with superstition, this tiny owl is the most commonly encountered member of its family. This is partly because it is often about during the day as well as at night. It is the only small owl without ear-tufts, and is generally brown with white or rufous spots. Unknown in Tobago but common in Trinidad, it is found in forests and semi-open country with scattered trees, including suburban areas. The call is a long series of even-toned hoots, varied sometimes by a musical 'chirruping' note.

Like most owls, the Pygmy-Owl nests in tree-hollows. It feeds on small creatures such as lizards and insects. Although it has rarely been recorded eating birds, its presence always provokes violent reactions from numbers of small birds, which gather round to mob and chase the little owl. Imitation of its call will thus tend to attract a number of other small birds. It nests in tree-holes, laying up to five white eggs, usually during the months of March to May.

◆ Common Pauraque   *Nyctidromus albicollis*

Length: 28 cm (11 inches)   **Family:** Nightjars

Common Pauraque

This species is probably the most common and widespread nightjar in our islands, although it is a bird which few people know well by sight. Entirely nocturnal in its activities, it can usually be seen at night beside the road with eyes shining in the headlight beams of cars. Cryptically patterned in brown, black and rufous, with some white in wings and tail, it relies on its camouflage to avoid attention during the day. Its habitat includes woodland and forest edges bordering savannahs, as at Waller Field. It is best recognised by its constantly repeated call, varying in style but usually a whistled phrase, e.g. *ker-whee-oo*.

Pauraques rest beside roads or paths at night, possibly because they can see their prey more easily, especially in moonlight. They hunt moths and other night insects, flying up from the ground to seize the prey in flight. Nesting takes place mainly in the dry season, when up to two creamy eggs are laid in a mere scrape among dead leaves on the ground. After hatching the young move away from the nest into cover, where they are fed and cared for by both parents.

Index